AMERICA AS EMPIRE

AMERICA

America's Destiny

AS EMPIRE

GLOBAL LEADER OR ROGUE POWER?

Jim Garrison

BERRETT-KOEHLER PUBLISHERS, INC.
San Francisco

BERRETT-KOEHLER PUBLISHERS, INC.
235 Montgomery Street, Suite 650
San Francisco, California 94104-2916
Tel: (415) 288-0260 Fax: (415) 362-2512 www.bkconnection.com

ORDERING INFORMATION

Quantity sales. Special discounts are available on quantity purchases by corporations, associations, and others. For details, contact the "Special Sales Department" at the Berrett-Koehler address above.

Individual sales. Berrett-Koehler publications are available through most bookstores. They can also be ordered direct from Berrett-Koehler: Tel: (800) 929-2929; Fax: (802) 864-7626; www.bkconnection.com

Orders for college textbook/course adoption use. Please contact Berrett-Koehler: Tel: (800) 929-2929; Fax: (802) 864-7626.

Orders by U.S. trade bookstores and wholesalers: Please contact Publishers Group West, 1700 Fourth Street, Berkeley, California 94710. Tel: (510) 528-1444; Fax (510) 528-3444.

Berrett-Koehler and the BK logo are registered trademarks of Berrett-Koehler Publishers, Inc.

PRINTED IN THE UNITED STATES OF AMERICA

Berrett-Koehler books are printed on long-lasting acid-free paper. When it is available, we choose paper that has been manufactured by environmentally responsible processes. These may include using trees grown in sustainable forests, incorporating recycled paper, minimizing chlorine in bleaching, or recycling the energy produced at the paper mill.

LIBRARY OF CONGRESS CATALOGING-IN-PUBLICATION DATA

Garrison, Jim, 1951–
    America as empire: global leader or rogue power? / by Jim Garrison.
        p. cm.
    Includes bibliographical references and index.
    ISBN 1-57675-281-X
        1. United States—Foreign relations —2001– 2. Balance of power. 3. Imperialism. 4. United States—Foreign relations—Moral and ethical aspects. 5. United States—Foreign relations. 6. Imperialism—History. I. Title.

E902.G37 2002
327.73—dc22   2003060684

FIRST EDITION

09 08 07 06 05 04   10 9 8 7 6 5 4 3 2 1

Copyediting by Sandra Beriss. Proofreading by Mary Lou Sumberg. Indexing by Rachel Rice.

This book is dedicated to GEORGES BERTHOIN, one of the truly wise ones, who has mentored me in the ways of statecraft and governance. It is to Georges that I owe the genesis of this book.

FOREWORD

SINCE SEPTEMBER 11, 2001, the perception—and the reality—is that the United States is no longer a nation among nations. It is an empire among nations. The short, stark, naked geopolitical history of the last hundred years is World War I, World War II, the Cold War, the American empire. This last is unlikely to be less important than the other three.

Although the United States has been an unrecognized empire for a long time, two years ago it was struck a mighty blow. The world saw that the American empire was not invulnerable. The shocking vulnerability of America shaped the recognition that it was both a mighty empire and that it had been severely wounded.

America's response was entirely predictable. Throughout history, all empires—including the great Roman Empire—had to give the unassailable impression that they were invincible. Whenever they were made to appear vulnerable, their invincibility had to be reasserted.

By hitting Afghanistan and Iraq, America was reestablishing its invincibility. As an empire—consciously or unconsciously—America had to do this, no matter what. Of course, it was done ostensibly to make the world safe from terrorists and from weapons of mass destruction. That is another practice of empires.

They justify their use of power by invoking lofty goals that are said to benefit everybody.

When Winston Churchill was a young officer in Africa at the end of the nineteenth century, he believed that the British Empire, under whose flag he served, had a historic, civilizing mission. The empire's purpose, he wrote, was to "give peace to warring tribes, to administer justice where all was violence, to strike the chains off the slave, to plant the seeds of commerce and learning." He asked himself, "What more beautiful idea can inspire human effort?" History has not been so generous.

What makes Jim Garrison's *America As Empire* so useful is that he places the global events beginning with September 11 into a much larger historical and philosophical context that helps immensely in understanding what is taking place in the world. This book is by no means anti-American. Indeed, it is because Garrison is so devoted to America's possible future, and to the possibilities of great leadership, that he makes the appeal for America to make the most of its leadership. And he makes it very clear that only the United States can lead.

After World War I, President Woodrow Wilson established the League of Nations. After World War II, President Roosevelt and President Truman established the United Nations and a host of international institutions that have provided the framework for global governance for the past sixty years. But these institutions were all developed before the advent of globalization, which now mandates a new examination of the kinds of institutions needed in an integrating world. Leadership reminiscent of Wilson and Roosevelt is now needed again.

If it attains this level of greatness, says Garrison, America could be the *final empire*, for what the next generation of global institutions could bequeath to the world is a democratic and integrated global system in which empire will no longer have a place. Garrison thus wants America to see itself as a *transitional empire*, one that uses its power to build mechanisms that will institutionalize America as partner rather than as empire. This is the theme that unites the entire book.

Garrison believes that the United States will dominate the twenty-first century as Rome dominated the first century. He asks not whether the United States will do this but rather whether it will *acknowledge* that this is what it is doing. Only if it takes up the mantle of leadership consciously will it be able to determine what kind of empire it will be.

Garrison asks this provocative question, "America at its moment of power, the world at its moment of integration: How will they come together? Will the world experience *pax Americana*, the American peace? Or *pox Americana*, the American plague?" How Americans and the world decide this will determine both America's legacy in history and the fate of the twenty-first century.

JOHN NAISBITT
Vienna, September 11, 2003

ACKNOWLEDGMENTS

I AM DEEPLY GRATEFUL to a range of people for their contributions to my thinking and in shaping the book as it traversed its pathway from free-ranging discussion to final manuscript. I am grateful first and foremost to Tom Rautenberg, one of the most elevated thinkers I know, for his abiding support and critical assistance from the very beginning, even before pen was put to paper. I am also grateful to Connie Zweig, who edited the manuscript with exquisite skill and artfulness. She is a master at her craft. Many thanks also to John Naisbitt both for his encouragement and for writing the foreword. John understands contemporary history with regard to the future with depth and perspicacity.

Others were genuinely helpful either by reading the various drafts and taking time to make comments or by offering suggestions through conversation along the way: Mahnaz Afkami, Antonio Arrelle, Lloyd Axworthy, Carl Bildt, Maria Livanos Cattaui, Paul Dietrich, Steve Donovan, Hans Peter Duerr, Gareth Evans, Millard Fuller, Luis Eduardo Garzon, Mark Gerzon, Khadija Haq, Dean and Shirley Harmison, HRH Prince Hassan ibn Tallil, Joan Holtzman, Will Hutton, Huguette LaBelle, David and Norma Lewis, Harriet Mouchly-Weiss, Irene Myers, Caroline Myss, Stephanie Pace Marshall, Berniece and Pat Patterson, Howard Perlmutter, Eduardo Ramos Gomez, Steve Rhinesmith, Jean-François Rischard, Mary Robinson, Kumar Rupesinghe, Roberto Savio, Bob Schwartz, Alexander Sellers, Jack Shenefield, Gordon Smith, Juan Somavia, George Soros, Tom Spencer, Steve Trevino, Jim Turner, Ken Wilber, Kathryn Williams, and Bill Ury.

I benefited enormously from the critical evaluations of the five readers provided by Berrett-Koehler: Mark Dowie, Gena Estes-Zolotar, David Korten, Jeff Kulick, and Ted Nace. They compelled me to seriously reexamine my underlying assumptions as well as my conclusions.

I am grateful to my colleagues at the State of the World Forum who assisted in myriad ways and encouraged me to give voice to such an important issue. Jim Hickman was the one right at the beginning who encouraged me to turn the original essay into a book, providing all sorts of good advice about doing so. Judi Karwan and Andy Krochalk did background research and generally kept the organizational boat afloat while I was preoccupied with writing. And a special thanks to Carman Melendrez, who was unsparing in her support as well as in supplying several themes that found their way into the manuscript.

My wife Claire and our two sons, Luke and Zachary, also need to be thanked for their encouragement as I squeezed whatever time available to write and rewrite and finally finish the manuscript. They put up with a lot and extended patient support all along the way. I have been blessed with a great family.

Finally, let me thank Candace Fuhrman, my literary agent, for her advice and wise counsel, and Steve Piersanti, the publisher of Berrett-Koehler, who from our first conversation demonstrated a magnanimity of spirit and openness of mind that, in the end, was the reason I went with his company.

The book was a pleasure to write. It literally burst out of me over just a few short months, almost fully formed. It came much more as an intuitive awareness about America than as a scientific investigation of impersonal data. The internal logic and the conclusions came from deep within me and are therefore mine alone. I trust that the reader finds them helpful in better understanding a very confusing and turbulent world. I ended the book with hope because that is the only way I can live.

JIM GARRISON
Mill Valley, California, September 2003

AMERICA AS EMPIRE

From Republic to Empire

I WRITE THIS BOOK AS A TENTH-GENERATION AMERICAN. My people on my father's side were Huguenots from southern France, an entrepreneurial Protestant group persecuted under King Louis XIV. In 1686 they fled to the New World, landing on the shores of North Carolina. They were among the earliest settlers of America, helping to shape colonial life through trading, farming, preaching, and writing. My forebears fought in the Revolutionary War and the Civil War. They joined the westward expansion as pioneers, and my immediate family arrived in California during the Great Depression of the 1930s. There, my father married my mother, a second-generation immigrant from Sicily.

My family's history has been America's history, for which I am grateful and proud. I deeply value the freedom to be uniquely myself without constraints imposed by government or class. America represents this freedom. It is this light that America shines on the world. I have lived this freedom, and in this sense, I am American to the very marrow of my bones.

I also write this book as a citizen of the world. My parents were Baptist missionaries in China, where I was born in 1951. They then moved to Taiwan, where I grew up attending a missionary school, speaking Chinese as fluently as English. As a child, I traveled throughout Asia, the Middle East, and Europe, coming to realize at an early age that the earth was indeed round and humanity rich with exotic diversity. I came back to the United States when I was fifteen and attended high school in San Jose, California, but then went abroad again for most of my university education, traveling through Africa, Latin America, Europe, and Russia. I have subsequently spent most of my professional life working and traveling internationally.

It is out of the interaction between my American roots and my international activities that this book arose, especially as I became aware of the dynamic power of the United States in the world and the growing alienation of the world from the United States. When I was a child in Taiwan in the 1950s, being American elicited respect and emulation, even envy. Now, fifty years later, being American elicits resentment and suspicion, even hatred. People used to think of America as a global leader. Now a majority of the world thinks of America as a rogue power. Why?

The answer to this question has to a large degree to do with what America has become: America has made the transition from republic to empire. It is no longer what it was. It was founded to be a beacon of light unto the nations, a democratic and egalitarian haven to which those seeking freedom could come. It has become an unrivaled empire among the nations, exercising dominion over them. How it behaves and what it represents have fundamentally changed. It used to represent freedom; now it represents power.

It was when I began to realize that my country had crossed the threshold from republic to empire that I began to study the history of empire—the only concept large and dynamic enough to explain what was going on. In many ways, this is the intent of the book, simply to provide a larger framework, a more complex metaphor with which to understand America and the world. *Republic* implies a single nation democratically governed, which is what America was founded to be. In contrast, the very essence of *empire* is one nation's control over other nations. Although America remains a republic inside its own borders, it has become an empire in relationship with the rest of the world. In this sense, America is an *imperial republic.*

The inordinate power of the United States disturbs people on the American left and excites people on the American right. Liberals are uncomfortable with the notion of an American empire because they are uneasy with the fact that the United States has so much power, especially military power. They would prefer that the United States simply be part of the community of nations—perhaps a first among equals but an equal nevertheless, using its power to further human welfare. Conservatives, on the other hand, are jubilant that America is finally breaking out of multilateral strictures and asserting its imperial prerogatives unilaterally around the world. For them, national self-interest, enforced by military supremacy, should be the guiding principle of U.S. policy. The liberal notion that the United States should confine its power within multilateral frameworks and the conservative desire to apply American power unilaterally for narrow self-interest are both inadequate. There is a deeper and more complex reality that needs to be noted.

Whatever qualms people may have about it, America *has* become an empire, and there is no turning back. As Heraclitus taught, one can never enter the same river twice. The transition from republic to empire is irreversible, like the metamorphosis from caterpillar to butterfly. Once power is attained, it is not surrendered. It is only exercised. The central question before America, therefore, is what it should do with all the power it has. How should it assert its authority and to what ends?

America should acknowledge—even celebrate—its transition to empire and the acquisition of global mastery. What began as a motley band of colonies 225 years ago is now not only the strongest nation in the world but the strongest nation in the history of the world. Americans should be justly proud of this achievement. It has been attained with enormous effort and at great cost.

The world, too, should modulate its antipathy toward America, realizing that America has become so powerful in part because it has been so benign. This might be a little hard to acknowledge for those who have felt the boot of American strength, but consider the three other major attempts at empire in the last century: the Soviet Union, Nazi Germany, and Imperial Japan. What would have happened if any of these empires had defeated the United States and established global hegemony? What would the world be like today if Nazi Germany and Japan had won the Second World War, or if the Soviets had won the Cold War? We should all breathe a sigh of relief that these eventualities never occurred and that a democratic nation committed to democratic values triumphed and established global dominion.

But having prevailed in the competition against these other empires and having achieved what they were denied, Americans should be aware that there are now enormous responsibilities to shoulder, both in relation to the United States itself and in relation to the world. An empire's reign can be long or short, its fate noble or tragic, depending on how astutely its leadership is exercised and its decisions are made. The exercise of power is highly unstable—especially the near-absolute power that empires represent. It provides opportunity, but it also corrupts. It demands wise action, but it also seduces to the dark side.

There are thus all sorts of dangers inherent in the exercise of power. Internally, the transition from republic to empire is almost always made at the cost of freedom. Power and freedom are contradictory and do not coexist comfortably. Freedom requires the limitation of power; power demands the surrender of freedom. This is something the ancient Athenians and Romans learned at great cost: democracy was the casualty of their empires. Americans must heed this ancient experience and painful truth. American freedoms are not eternally bestowed, but must with each generation and circumstance be reevaluated and preserved. Freedom is lost far more easily than it is gained, especially when it is surrendered for the sake of greater power.

Externally, empires incite insurrection. No nation wants to be ruled, especially those that have just been liberated, such as Afghanistan and Iraq. Maintaining dominion is therefore a very tricky challenge, particularly in a world of instantaneous communication and porous borders, in which information and people can move about virtually unimpeded and small actions can have large and unexpected effects. This was the lesson of September 11. Empires have many enemies and few friends. Americans must know this as they rule, especially in obscure places far from American shores.

To achieve greatness, an empire needs a transcendental vision that can unite all its disparate elements within an overarching purpose. It must aspire to a mission that the entire empire can join together to achieve. It must be fundamentally constructive, not destructive.

This is the deeper purpose of this book: to challenge Americans at their point of empire to articulate a vision for the world that is worthy of the power they now wield over the world. This vision must transcend self-interest and embrace the whole. In order to achieve this, Americans must remember that even though their country now represents power, it has historically symbolized freedom. Can the vision that built the American republic now guide America the empire?

History teaches that great empires are constructed not simply through military might but by building institutions that are perceived by the governed as just and fair. The common interest of the empire as a whole must supercede the national interest of the dominant state in order for the empire to endure. The great paradox of empire is that stewardship is far more powerful than force in maintaining control.

Sixty years ago, President Roosevelt and President Truman achieved this level of greatness, as did President Woodrow Wilson the generation before them. They defeated world fascism and contained communism by ensuring that the United States had the strongest military in the world. But at the same time, they founded the United Nations, established the Bretton Woods institutions, implemented the Marshall Plan, and created NATO. Taken together, these institutions ushered in a new postcolonial international system. They blended American interests with the interests of the common good to create a new world order. American strength thus served political aspirations that were welcomed by the international community as beneficial.

Six decades later, the forces of globalization have made the institutions built then anachronistic. Today, the world is in a new state of crisis. The greatest difference between today and sixty years ago, however, is that then there was an undeniable crisis: a world at war. Now, although the crisis is of similar magnitude, it is evolving more like an accident in slow motion. The world's problems range from global warming, loss of biodiversity, overfishing, deforestation, and water scarcity to persistent poverty, organized crime, drugs, terrorism, overpopulation, failed states, and HIV AIDS. As all of these problems press down on us, the prevailing system of international institutions and the system of nation-states are simply incapable of effective response. The planet is thus quite literally on a collision course with itself. Yet strangely, the totality of the danger is not yet apparent. World leaders do little more than talk about it. Most are simply in denial.

The opportunity for America in this situation is to ask itself anew what it can do about the needs of the global commons. How can it proactively lead the world out of the present crisis? How can it revitalize the international order and lead in the development of innovative solutions to global problems? What global institutions need to be established to ensure that democracy and prosperity, along with American primacy, prevail in the twenty-first century?

What both Americans and the world must internalize is that no one but the United States is even remotely capable of leading this effort. The United Nations is weak and bureaucratically paralyzed. Other powers that may one day serve as regional sources of stability and order—such as the European Union, Russia, China, India, or Brazil—are themselves either unformed, unstable, or not yet sufficiently coherent. The myriad number of new international initiatives and institutions coming from the nongovernmental sector have high aspirations but remain fragile, underfunded, and only marginally effective.

In just a few decades, this situation may be completely different. But right now, only the United States has the capacity, the traditions, the reach, and the will to lead at the global level. There is literally no one else to do it. This means that the highest vision for the American empire must be to serve the need for effective management of the global system in which all of humanity now participates.

The greatest temptation at the moment of power is to be seduced by the dark side, or in arrogance to dispense with "the vision thing," as President George Bush, Sr., once put it, and then simply use power for the sake of gaining even more power. The question before the United States is whether it will allow the magnitude of its power to eclipse the light by which it was founded or whether it will use its power to shine an even greater light. Will it seek mastery to dominate or mastery to serve? This is a crucially important distinction. If it uses its power to build democracy at the global level with the same genius with which it built democracy at the national level, then the United States could leave a legacy so powerful that the world will become knitted into a singularity of democracy and freedom. The possibility for a successor empire could then be superceded by the demands of a single global system.

To do this, America must consciously view itself as a *transitional empire*, one whose destiny at this moment is to act as midwife to a democratically governed global system. Its great challenge is not to dominate but to catalyze. It must use its great strength and democratic heritage to establish integrating institutions and mechanisms to manage the emerging global system so that its own power is subsumed by the very edifice it helps to build.

President Wilson established the League of Nations out of the ashes of World War I. Presidents Roosevelt and Truman established a new international order after World War II. America must now build the third iteration of global governance. If it attains this level of greatness, it could become the *final empire,* for it will have bequeathed to the world a democratic and integrated global system in which empire will no longer have a place or perform a role.

This is the challenge before America: to manifest a destiny of both light and power at the level of global affairs. It is ultimately a challenge about how high it will cast its sights, about what kind of vision it will manifest as it leads a world fraught with crises. The deepest question is whether Americans will have the political and moral strength to rise to this occasion, and whether the world will then accept the leadership that the United States will provide.

1

America and the World

THE UNITED STATES HAS BECOME what it was founded not to be. Established as a haven for those fleeing the abuse of power, it has attained and now wields nearly absolute power. It has become an empire. This is meant as a statement of fact, not a judgment of national character. It is a way of understanding America, not an indictment against American policy. Indeed, by opening up the possibility of viewing the United States as an empire, one opens up a far larger frame of reference to understand America's history, role in the world, and future responsibilities.

WHAT IS AN EMPIRE? According to the *Oxford Dictionary*, an empire is "a group of countries ruled by a single supreme authority." The word itself comes from the old French word *empire*, meaning imperial rule. It is derived from the Latin term *imperium*, meaning to rule, to command. The historian Alexander Motyl defines empire as "a hierarchically organized political system with a hublike structure—a rimless wheel—within which a core elite and state dominate peripheral elites and societies by serving as intermediaries for their significant interactions and by channeling resource flows from the periphery to the core and back to the periphery."[1] The historian Michael Doyle provides a more behavioristic definition: "Effective control, whether formal or informal, of a subordinated society by an imperial society."[2]

Empires are thus relationships of influence and control by one state over a group of lesser states. This can take a variety of forms, ranging from territorial annexation and direct political rule to economic domination and diplomatic oversight. Empires are as old as history itself and characterize the earliest stages of human development. For reasons deeply buried in the human psyche and soul, human beings have always competed against one another, and the victors have invariably established dominion over the vanquished and exploited that relationship to their own benefit. Almost all peoples on earth have at some point expanded and conquered or contracted and been conquered—often many times over and in a variety of combinations.

Of all governing institutions, empires are the most complex and extensive. Empire stands at the apex of the social, economic, and political pyramid, integrating all the peoples, nations, and institutions within it into a unified order. An empire well run is the greatest accolade a nation can receive. An empire squandered is the most damning legacy it can leave behind.

FROM THE FALL OF THE BERLIN WALL TO THE FALL OF THE TWIN TOWERS   Policy analyst Michael Ignatieff states in his article "American Empire" in the *New York Times Sunday Magazine* that the United States "is the only nation that polices the world through five global military commands; maintains more than a million men and women at arms on four continents; deploys carrier battle groups on watch in every ocean; guarantees the survival of countries from Israel to South Korea; drives the wheels of global trade and commerce; and fills the hearts and minds of an entire planet with its dreams and desires."[3]

Surprisingly, the inordinate and unique power of the United States was not immediately recognized when the Berlin Wall came down in 1989 and the Soviet Union disintegrated. While a few observers recognized that America had entered what columnist Charles Krauthammer called a *unipolar moment,* most commentators predicted that the demise of the Soviet Union and end of the Cold War would lead to a return to the age-old balance of powers.

Such a view was completely understandable. The last fifteen hundred years of European history have been essentially multipolar. The major European powers incessantly competed against one another without any single power ever gaining undue advantage, whether during the medieval era of city-states or the modern era of nation-states. Even Britain at its prime during the nineteenth century was constrained by France, Russia, Spain, and Germany. During the reign of Queen Victoria, from 1837 to 1901, which marked the apex of British imperial power, Britain had to fight seventy-two separate military campaigns to keep its rivals at bay and its colonial holdings intact. The very notion of *realpolitik* is predicated upon the assumption of a balance of power between major states.

That the United States broke out of this multipolar framework to attain unipolar global dominance is an extraordinary achievement in the annals of history, not attained by any power since Rome two thousand years ago. Because the world had gotten so used to thinking in multilateral and multipolar terms, it took some time for the novelty of the historical situation to sink in.

In his book *The Rise and Fall of the Great Powers,* published in 1988, Yale historian Paul Kennedy went so far as to predict the relative decline of the United States due to "imperial overstretch." Talk of American weakness dominated the 1992 U.S. presidential elections, with the ultimate victor, Bill Clinton, focusing on fixing the ailing American economy while his rival for the Democratic nomination, Paul Tsongas, repeatedly declared, "The Cold War is over and Japan won."

Margaret Thatcher expressed the commonly held view that the world would evolve into three regional groups: one based on the dollar, one on the mark, one on the yen. Henry Kissinger solemnly predicted the emergence of a multipolar world. Asians, along with some American Asian enthusiasts such as James Fallows, spoke exuberantly of the rise of a "Pacific century."

The Clinton administration (1993 to 2001) was essentially a transitional period when the United States was emerging as what French Foreign Minister Hubert Vedrine called a "hyperpower," but was still essentially multilateralist and collaborative in its mentality and behavior. The title of Richard Haass's book, *The Reluc-*

tant Sheriff, published in 1998, summarized in advance the legacy Clinton was to leave behind. Clinton's main focus was the integration of the global economy under American hegemony, but he seldom used the power America had at its disposal, seeking rather to work collegially with American allies on issues of common concern.

While believing that the United States was the "indispensable power," as then-Secretary of State Madeleine Albright was fond of putting it, Clinton exercised this indispensability with discretion. He initiated limited military actions against Iraq and the Sudan and led the European coalition in Kosovo, but by and large he remained committed to multilateralism and to upholding the international treaties negotiated by his predecessors. These included the Comprehensive Nuclear Test Ban Treaty and the Antiballistic Missile Treaty, signed by Presidents Kennedy and Nixon, to limit America's nuclear capabilities. Clinton also negotiated and signed the Kyoto Protocol on Global Warming that would constrain the emission of hydrofluorocarbons into the atmosphere. All these treaties framed U.S. strategic interests in the context of collective security considerations.

In general, the 1990s were marked by a strong commitment to international law, working within the context of the U.N. system, and upholding preexistent treaty obligations. America was certainly the senior partner in all deliberations but the emphasis by Americans and the larger world community was on the importance of partnership as much as on American seniority.

Then came the events of September 11, 2001. The response by the new Bush administration dramatically altered the former equilibrium by heightening asymmetries already there but unobserved because unexercised. Right at the point it was emerging as the undisputed superpower, the United States was attacked unexpectedly and with devastating impact by nonstate actors virtually invisible to the American intelligence apparatus. In one of the strangest incidents of modern history, a nation that thought itself invulnerable was made, without warning, completely vulnerable. Its response was to strike back with an overwhelming application of military power in Afghanistan and Iraq, making it clear to friend and foe alike that there is one undisputed military power in the world: the United States of America.

Since September 11, the United States has emphasized national security concerns and preemptive military responses in a war on terrorism that President Bush declared the highest priority for American domestic and foreign policy. Multilateralism, where the coalition defines the mission, has been replaced by unilateralism, where the mission defines the coalition. Deterrence, where there is an assumed balance of power, has been superceded by preemptive strikes, where the United States hits first against potential adversaries.

THE INVASION OF IRAQ   The events of 9/11 reframed global affairs within the context of national security and the war on terrorism. The invasion of Iraq reframed global affairs yet again within the reality of overwhelming American military might. What is extraordinary is that the United States exercised its strength and global reach by seizing the most strategic area in the Middle East.

U.S. military forces now occupy the area along the Tigris-Euphrates river basin. This is where the Neolithic revolution and the domestication of plants and animals began ten thousand years ago. This is where the first human civilization at Sumer, in the environs of present-day Baghdad, developed six thousand years ago, and where the first empire under Sargon the Great, also around Baghdad, held sway five thousand years ago. This is where Abraham was born. It is where, closely to the west, Judaism and Christianity had their origins, with Islam originating just to the south. Zoroastrianism and Baha'i arose to the east. The Tigris-Euphrates river basin is the cradle of Arab civilization and the site of the early Muslim Abbassid dynasty. The armies of Alexander the Great marched here, as did the Roman legions and the hordes of Genghis Khan.

There is no place in the entire world more steeped in history, more complex in its politics, more charged in its religious fervor than the Tigris-Euphrates river basin. For the United States to take control of this region at America's moment of vulnerability and power is utterly profound. America reacted to a blow and demonstrated world dominion by seizing the most sacred and fought over soil in the history of the world.

What disturbed the world most about the U.S. invasion of Iraq was the manner in which it was done. There was none of the finesse with which President Bush, Sr., had mobilized an international coalition and utilized the resources and legitimacy of the United Nations during the earlier Iraqi operation, Desert Storm, in 1991. Instead, George W. Bush went into Iraq belligerently, threatening and then marginalizing the United Nations, invading essentially alone with the British, despite widespread international public opposition.

The vindictive and highly militarized response by President Bush to 9/11 provided the world with an experience of America that was aggressive, ruthless, cynical, and dogmatic. In his book *Special Providence*, policy analyst Walter Russell Mead calls this the "Jacksonian" tradition of American history, named after President Andrew Jackson, whose administration was characterized by fighting the Indians and taming the West during the 1830s. It was a time when the world was cast in black and white and the aim was to defeat the enemy without mercy, giving no quarter. The Jacksonian tradition is one of "us against them," and is infused by patriotic fervor, a culture of honor, and military pride.

Mead also notes other traditions: the "Hamiltonian," named after Alexander Hamilton, the first U.S. secretary of the treasury, representing the American interest in developing commerce and trade; the "Jeffersonian," named after President Thomas Jefferson, deeply concerned with protecting democracy and human rights; and the "Wilsonian," named after President Woodrow Wilson, heralding world-changing political ideals. All of these traditions conjoin to produce the totality of the American political expression, in terms of both its domestic and its foreign policy.

Prior to 9/11, the United States was in a classic Hamiltonian phase. President Clinton focused his entire administration on the economy: balancing the budget, eliminating the deficit, forging free trade agreements, and presiding over robust economic growth. The U.S. economy was better tended during his watch than perhaps at any time in modern American history, even considering the collapse of the high-technology economy and the stock market at the end of his administration in 2000. Americans were generally positive about the world, optimistic about the future and content with the multilateral framework of international relations in which America operated.

In the aftermath of 9/11, America experienced a fundamental reversal of emotions and perceptions. Almost overnight, the Jacksoninan impulse gripped the president, and under his leadership, the American public. What had been a world-centric orientation was radically replaced by nation-centric tribalism. Multilateralism was replaced by unilateralism, global diplomacy by military force, and congeniality with confrontation.

While the starkness of this transformation startled the world, it was actually a very natural response. Under the impact of a trauma, psychologists have long observed that people and groups can experience a radical reversal of values. After major disasters such as earthquakes, floods, civil unrest, or wars, for instance, there is generally a heightened commitment to the community as well as excesses of looting. Normally law-abiding citizens are capable of extraordinary acts of sacrifice and heroism as well as egregious acts of lawlessness. There is something about experiencing trauma, especially among large numbers of people, which activates our altruistic as well as our aggressive impulses.

Both heroism and widespread looting took place in the aftermath of the fall of Baghdad during the U.S. invasion of Iraq. It also occurred in the aftermath of the Loma Prieta earthquake south of San Francisco in 1989, and in the aftermath of the Northridge earthquake in Los Angeles in 1994. It is also a pattern found in antiquity, and was chronicled by the historian Thucydides in Athens after a major outbreak of plague during the fourth century B.C.

If one considers the magnitude of the trauma inflicted on the American psyche by the attack of 9/11, coupled with the fact that it was in its essence a military attack against the United States, it is both normal and predictable that the initial response was to come together with a heightened sense of community as well as to respond with belligerence. There were acts of heroism by the police and firefighters at the World Trade Center. There was also some looting. Patriotic fervor soared across America and the nation came together in mutual support and solidarity not seen since the Second World War. This communal feeling coalesced around healing the nation, rebuilding New York, and getting back at the perpetrators. An overwhelming number of Americans felt the need to come together as a nation and to strike back. President Bush molded this emotion with his declaration of a war against terrorism.

The United States then proceeded to break out of the norms of international law and procedures and conduct its own retribution. President Bush often referred to himself as a sheriff heading up a posse. At some level, it felt good for Americans to brush the United Nations aside and go into the Arab world and "kick ass."

In this sense, Saddam Hussein was the occasion, not the reason for the invasion of Iraq. This point was noted by Thomas Friedman in his column in the *New York Times*. He observed that the attack of September 11 was the "real reason" the United States invaded. As Friedman put it, removing the Taliban from Afghanistan was not enough. America needed to go out into the Arab world and clobber somebody else, and Saddam was it. "Smashing Saudi Arabia or Syria would have been fine. But we hit Saddam for one simple reason: because we could, and because he deserved it, and because he was right in the heart of that world."[4] All other reasons were of secondary importance, including the issue of weapons of mass destruction and the alleged link between Iraq and al-Qaeda.

What came together in the aftermath of 9/11 was the psycho-emotional need for vengeance with the geostrategic opportunity to demonstrate to the world the overwhelming military might of the United States. Understanding and responding to this, the Bush administration hit the Arab world with power, precision, and decisiveness, seizing control of a region that had been a thorn in the side of the United States for decades.

The effects of this attitude and this action reverberated around the world. At one level, there was mimicry. The Russians renewed their efforts to crush Chechnya, the Indonesians invaded Acheh,

Israel increased military pressure on the Palestinians, and India mobilized against Pakistan, all of them citing the U.S. war on terrorism as a legitimating model for their own behavior.

At another level, world public opinion reacted sharply to the aggressiveness of the Bush administration and dramatically questioned the integrity of America's leadership. The invasion of Iraq in defiance of overwhelming opposition indicated to many that America, the global leader, had become America, the rogue imperium. Since the war, anti-American sentiment continues to rise virtually all over the world, including in Europe, traditionally America's strongest ally.

QUESTIONS OF EMPIRE   At the core of the current dialectic between America and the world is the issue of where the center of gravity for international affairs should be: the United States or the United Nations. This presents America and the world with a fundamental choice: Should the world be ruled by an empire or by the community of nations?

At the end of World War II, the United States established the United Nations out of self-interest. Today, the United States disregards the United Nations out of a very different notion of self-interest. The United States founded the United Nations to help prevent war among the nations. The United States now considers the United Nations to be weak, corrupt, inefficient, and bureaucratic, unable to exert leadership in critical issues pertaining to international security and rogue states. The United States has thus marginalized the United Nations and has assumed the role of arbiter and enforcer in the international security domain.

At the same time, the United Nations represents to most people—including most Americans—the desire for a community of nations, governed by the sanctity of international law and cooperating through dialogue and consensus. Whatever its flaws, it is the carrier of the deep human aspiration for peace. U.S. disparagement of the United Nations and its willingness to act alone in spite of it are thus of deep concern to the international public.

But what the United Nations and the larger world community must come to grips with is the reality that the United States is no longer a nation among nations. It is an empire among nations, an absolutely key concept in understanding why America is acting the way it is and why the international community is so concerned. America has emerged as an unchallenged superpower, controlling countries and institutions all around the world. As such, it can and will assume certain imperial prerogatives, particularly in the immediate aftermath of September 11 and because there is now no countervailing power to challenge it.

Empires invariably reserve the right to act in their own interests, precisely because, from an imperial point of view, might makes right. In assessing American actions, the world must remember that military power is the beginning and the end of empire and that empires seek to weaken international law and multilateral institutions in order to maximize maneuverability and maintain dominion. The master strategy of empire is to divide and conquer.

The confusion and resentment toward the United States are due in part to the fact that many in the secular world were lulled into believing, with philosopher Francis Fukuyama, that when the Cold War ended we had somehow reached the "end of history," and empires and other nasty things would no longer occur. But with the highly militarized foreign policy formation of the Bush administration, to say nothing about the general crisis of the world situation, we have been shocked to discover that here history is again, and it has been its lack of preparedness for this that constitutes a major part of the world's predicament.

This is another reason for asserting that the United States is an empire: it is a continuation of history as we have known it. Through its own sheer force and through mediating institutions such as the World Bank and International Monetary Fund, along with numerous other bilateral and multilateral institutions, the United States now controls more nations in more ways than any nation in history.

Paradoxically, while the American empire is a continuation of history, history itself is moving beyond empire. It is actually in the penultimate stage of development before full global integration.

This is the critical concept in understanding why the United States needs to consider itself as a *transitional empire*. It will be the *final empire* by choice or as victim. What history demands, even empires must address, or they are consumed.

Why will it be the final empire? Because the world is rapidly becoming an integrated system under the impact of economic globalization and the technology of instantaneous communication. In an integrated system, it is the system itself, not a particular part of it, that is of crucial importance. The United States is strong now because the global system has not yet been fully built. Once it has been, U.S. power will be absorbed within the larger whole. It is America's historic challenge to lead in building the very system that will replace it.

In an integrating world, leadership must change from domination to stewardship. Cultural nuances and social disparities matter far more than military might, and issues of ethnicity and religion go far deeper than the power of the state. Governance cannot be exercised successfully simply by the application of precision warfare. Brute force does not make friends and cannot change a person's mind.

There is increasingly a *civilizational* context for governance that needs to be taken into account. The international community requires leadership that is sensitive to societal and cultural differences as well as to political and economic conditions. It needs leadership that will foster the integrating institutions necessary to bring these complex factors together for the equitable management of the global system. Diversity can only be integrated with patience and compromise. All voices must be honored and consensus built in the context of mutual respect and international norms and procedures. Leadership in this context is successful more through influence than by coercion, more through empowerment of others than by exerting power over others.

The interplay between America's power—unsurpassed, militarily oriented, and unilaterally directed—and the needs of an integrating world—highly diverse, culturally conditioned, and requiring a spirit of stewardship in order to be governed effectively—is the framework in which the American empire will live out its unique destiny. Both America and the world, for better or for worse, will be shaped by how this destiny unfolds.

In all probability, the United States will dominate the twenty-first century as Rome dominated the first. The critical question is not *whether* it will do this but whether it will *acknowledge* that this is what it is doing. Only if it consciously takes up the mantle of leadership will it be able to determine the kind of empire it will be. This decision will determine its own fate as well as the fate of the earth for decades to come. To the degree to which it remains faithful to its founding vision and is informed by the lessons that can be gleaned from the experiences of earlier imperial powers, it will endure.

America at its moment of power, the world at its moment of integration. How will they come together? Will the world experience *pax Americana*, the American peace? Or *pox Americana*, the American plague? Will imperial America be remembered as the architect of the world's first global order or as a tragedy of epic proportions? These are the great questions of our time and the exploration of this book.

2

A Mighty Fortress on Shifting Sands

As the twenty-first century gets under way, the primacy of American power is one of the few undisputed truths of international affairs. The United States dominates the world militarily with 436 bases in North America and Europe, 186 in the Pacific and Southeast Asia, 14 in Latin America and the Caribbean, 7 in the Middle East, and 1 in South Asia, 647 altogether. It has bases or base rights in over forty countries around the world and a navy with an array of aircraft carrier task forces that dominate every ocean. The U.S. Air Force has a presence on six of the world's continents.

The United States has developed an unrivaled mastery of high-technology weaponry that has radically redefined the meaning of modern warfare and includes a massive nuclear arsenal on hair-trigger alert, capable of destroying any enemy completely and the world several times over. It has the military capability of fighting on several fronts simultaneously and is building a national missile defense system to protect the American mainland from sneak missile attack. It almost certainly will weaponize space within the next decade, giving the United States essentially complete military control over global communications.

In addition to these overt displays of power, the United States also applies what journalist Robert Kaplan calls *supremacy by stealth*. This includes covert operations implemented by special forces operatives in over 170 nations worldwide, with an average of nine "quiet professionals," as the army calls them, on each mission. The objective of these operations is to gather intelligence, make local contacts, and ensure that U.S. policies are implemented either legally or extralegally. Thousands of operations are conducted each year. Especially since 9/11, U.S. military and intelligence personnel have burrowed deeply into foreign intelligence agencies, military forces, and police units around the world.

Complementing this, the U.S. National Security Agency and other agencies monitor all phone calls and much electronic communication to and from the United States. Working principally with British intelligence abroad, most of the world's international telephonic and electronic communications are monitored, and have been for years. The United States currently deploys over one hundred national security satellites that provide constant global intelligence.

To develop and maintain these capacities, the United States currently spends more on military outlays than the next fifteen to twenty biggest nations of the world combined. Moreover, Washington is not giving anyone the opportunity to catch up, spending three times more on military research and development than the next six nations combined, which is more than Germany and Britain spend on their militaries in total.

This is all being accomplished by spending merely 3.5 percent of America's gross domestic product, less than a third of what it spent during World War II. As the historian Paul Kennedy put it in 2002, recanting his declinist theories of the 1990s, "Nothing has ever existed like this disparity of power; nothing. Being Number One at great cost is one thing; being the world's single superpower on the cheap is astonishing."[1] With these capacities, and with American troops stationed on every major continent and in nearly every region, the United States is the indispensable component of international stability and the guarantor of democratic institutions around the world.

The United States is also the wealthiest and most economically robust economy in the world, twice the size of its closest rival, Japan. The state of California alone has risen to become the world's fifth largest economy, ahead of France and just behind Great Britain. The United States as a whole produces roughly 30 percent of the total global economic output, more than Japan, Germany, and Great Britain combined. The United States is also the most favored destination in the world for foreign firms, and attracts roughly one-third of all foreign direct investment.

The U.S. economy is as strong as it is because the United States is the country best positioned to take advantage of economic globalization. Indeed, it dominates global communications, the world's financial markets, and the international financial institutions that govern economic globalization, setting the rules and serving as the engine of the global economy.

Both American military and economic strength are rooted in America's position as the world's leading scientific and technological power. Most of the major developments in the computer industry, including the Internet itself, have come from the United States over the past five decades. The exploration of space has been dominated by American technology, most spectacularly demonstrated by the manned landing on the moon in 1969, and continuing with the Hubble space telescope and the development of the International Space Station. And although many other nations compete scientifically and technologically, the United States continues to be the preferred destination for scientifically trained workers from around the world. It is a major player in virtually every sphere of technological development.

The United States also exerts cultural dominance over the world through the seductive power of its music, movies, television shows, sports, automobiles, fashions, and fast-food chains. English is the common language of global economics, politics, science, entertainment, and the Internet. American culture has in fact become as extensive as and often synonymous with globalization itself, with American products, icons, images, and fads permeating every country open to free market economics. Traditional societies and non-Western cultures resist but in the end are overwhelmed by brand Americana, largely because products American are embraced by the young. American culture sets the pace for the emerging global culture.

Finally, each year the United States allows far more legal immigration than any other nation in the world, drawing to itself now, as it has for more than two centuries, the intellectual and creative talent of the human race restless for freedom and economic opportunity. Through its leading academic institutions, it trains the best minds in the world, welcoming, generating, and shaping the largest pool of human talent and creativity in the world and in the annals of history. An overwhelming number of Nobel Prizes are awarded to Americans, and most of the laureates speak with foreign accents.

Without historical precedent, the United States dominates the world in the military, economic, scientific, technological, and cultural domains *simultaneously*. Previous great powers were dominant in one or two domains but not in others. At the height of the British Empire during the 1870s, for example, the British navy was unsurpassed and ruled the waves. But both Russia and France spent more on their militaries, deployed more troops, and had larger arsenals. The 24 percent of gross domestic product Great Britain commanded among the six largest powers was matched by the United States, which also had 24 percent. Russia and Germany were close behind.

Just a few years ago, during the Cold War, the Soviet Union managed to retain overall military parity with the United States, deploy more troops in the field, and stay competitive in the space race. Yet today, the United States has no serious rival in any critical domain of power. All roads lead to New York and Washington, D.C. Together, they dominate a turbulent world.

The *unipolar moment* noted by writer Charles Krauthammer in 1991 has become a *unipolar era* as the twenty-first century begins.

POTENTIAL COMPETITORS   About this state of affairs, German political commentator Josef Joffe writes, "The history books say that Mr. Big always invites his own demise. Nos. 2, 3, and 4 will gang up on him, form countervailing alliances, and plot his down-fall. That happened to Napoleon, as it happened to Louis XIV and the mighty Hapsburgs, to Hitler and to Stalin. Power begets superior counterpower; it's the oldest rule of world politics."[2]

Some analysts believe that the European Union might become big enough to counter the United States. When its latest enlargement is complete, Europe will comprise more than five hundred million people from Spain to the Baltics and from Ireland to the Balkans. Europeans certainly have both the tradition and the experience for world leadership and in time Europe probably could become a competing power, especially if the United States mismanages its dominion and recedes or collapses—something that is not immediately probable but also is not beyond the realm of possibility. It all depends on what decisions America makes over the next several decades.

Still, it is not likely in the short term that the EU will develop military capabilities that are competitive with those of the United States. Nor will it wield them coherently, as a unitary state independent of the United States and NATO, which the United States established and still dominates. Today, the EU struggles to put together a sixty-thousand-strong rapid-deployment force designed for small-scale operations such as crisis management, humanitarian relief, and peacekeeping. Its military spending is down, not up.

More fundamentally, western Europe has spent the past fifty years prospering safely behind the military and nuclear shield of the United States. It has had the luxury of concentrating on integrating with eastern Europe and establishing a region where war is no longer a practical possibility. Europe has no incentive to upset or destroy the benefits it derives from this protection by the United States, whatever the rhetoric individual Europeans employ against the American behemoth. The hundreds of billions of euros that Europe has saved by not having to undertake its own defense for the most part have been invested in social programs that give the Europeans the most comprehensive and generous social welfare systems in the world.

There is currently in Europe little public or political support to exchange social services for a military buildup and scant support for competing geostrategically with the United States. Instead, Europe is developing its identity as a union. It will, over time, develop a clearer identity and ethos of its own. To some degree, these will develop antagonistically against the United States. In Will Hutton's book *The World We Are In,* he analyzes the diverging identities, values, and social contracts that are taking shape in Europe and the United States. They are evolving in fundamentally different and even opposing directions, and this will make Europe increasingly a contrary voice to American intentions and policies in the world.

Because of this increasing divergence between Europe and America, what is possible, and indeed desirable, is a major role for Europe *with* the United States in constructing the global institutions necessary for the effective management of the global system. However, in the emerging American-dominated world order, the Euro-American relationship may not be the mainstay it once was. What happens will be based as much on choices America makes as on choices Europe makes. How it will play out over time is impossible to say, but a united Europe will only grow stronger politically, economically, and militarily. And deeply embedded in its strength will be the memory of empire.

There are some who predict that China could assume a global countervailing role against the United States, but this is unlikely to happen for a number of reasons. China is the oldest continuous civilization in the world, going back some five thousand years. The Chinese have learned over time that it is better not to have serious imperial ambitions. They value culture more than dominance, commerce more than territory. This is perhaps the key to China's longevity.

China certainly has been invaded by expanding empires, but it has never expanded to build an extended empire itself. Unlike the Europeans, for example, the Chinese never sent imperial troops to Africa, Europe, or the Western Hemisphere. China has always stayed essentially inside its traditional borders and cultivated the "Middle Kingdom" itself, occasionally venturing out to the northeast to Korea and Japan and to the south to Vietnam and Malaysia, but never for long and never, like the Japanese, across the Pacific.

Tibet is in all probability the extent of any serious Chinese imperial ambitions, along with its desire for unification with Taiwan, which it views as an essential step toward national integration rather than an act of aggression toward another sovereign state.

Even if the current Chinese leadership were to dispense with this wisdom, Chinese intelligence officials project that by 2020, China, under the most optimistic scenarios, will only possess between one-third and one-half of U.S. capabilities. More than 50 percent of the Chinese labor force is currently employed in agriculture, in contrast with less than 3 percent in the United States. Relatively little of its economy is geared toward high technology, with the United States spending over twenty times as much on technological research. The Chinese military is antiquated by U.S. standards, even if its missiles are capable of hitting the American homeland.

China's overarching preoccupation is with economic growth, and in this sphere it is emerging as a global power. But China will almost certainly be plagued by economic and political turbulence as it transitions to a market economy. In China today there is certainly economic dynamism, but there is also pervasive dissatisfaction with a stultified bureaucracy. A persistent pattern in Chinese history is the uprising of angry peasants against corrupt leaders, leading to revolution.

Unrest from within will increasingly be matched by pressure from without. This is a point made by Thomas Friedman in *The Lexus and the Olive Tree:* that the phenomenon of globalization is antithetical to centralized and authoritarian governments. They cannot long endure against the decentralizing, and eventually, democratizing effect of instantaneous communications and interdependent economic and financial markets. The form of government that will replace China's current one-party, Marxist-oriented government, and the processes by which this change will be transacted, are uncertain, especially because over 1.2 billion people are involved.

In the meantime, China will at most play a role antagonistic to American interests in the region. China needs America as an enemy for domestic cohesion, and the strictures of its Marxist ideology do not allow much beyond an uneasy coexistence with a superpower that it wants to emulate but cannot become. China certainly wants to play an active role in any of the councils deliberating on global concerns. It should and will play such a role, but at least over the next several decades, it will do so as a regional rather than a global player.

Finally, none of America's potential rivals—China, Germany, Japan, Russia—could dramatically augment their militaries without becoming immediate threats to their own neighbors, thus triggering regional balancing mechanisms long before any serious threat was posed to the United States. If Germany unilaterally rearmed, all of Europe would be destabilized and the very fabric of the European Union threatened. Japanese rearmament would cause equally serious repercussions throughout East Asia. Russian rearmament would arouse dramatic concern in both Asia and Europe. If China, surrounded by Russia, India, Indonesia, Australia, and Japan, took such actions, it would trigger multiregional balancing responses.

More fundamentally, the history of great powers balancing one another generally involves a coalition of strong nations grouping together to prevent an upstart power from gaining advantage, as happened with Napoleon after the French Revolution. The situation today is the reverse: American dominance *is* the status quo. Not only that, Japan and Germany are close allies of the United States and have derived significant benefits from that relationship. Russia and China are weakened states incapable of mobilizing the kind of coalition necessary to counter U.S. power. They have far more to gain from a friendly relationship with America than from enmity. In any case, there is no historical precedent for a group of subordinate states joining to topple a dominant power once the dominant power has emerged as such, which is the situation today. It is only when the dominant power decays and weakens that this is possible.

No serious military challenge to the United States is thus likely to emerge for the foreseeable future. Especially in the aftermath of Iraq, no country, or group of countries, will deliberately maneuver itself into a situation in which it will have to contend with the focused military might of the United States. At the same time, the world finds it frightening to have so much power concentrated in the hands of one state, especially when the United States so aggressively goes its own way. But so broad is the acquiescence to U.S. dominance that most major powers, whatever their rhetoric about America, actually have been reducing in relative and sometimes absolute terms the amounts they spend on their own militaries. China is an important exception. Quite simply, no one wants to compete against the American military behemoth.

The absence of a serious rival further empowers the United States in its quest for global dominion. The Cold War demonstrated the enervating drain of resources, attention, and energy that such a rivalry compels. From the end of World War II until the fall of the Berlin Wall in 1989, the United States was faced with a power that embraced an antithetical ideology and could, if unchecked, conquer all of Europe and much of Asia. For nearly five decades, the United States protected the free world against this "Communist menace." It spent 5 percent to 14 percent of its GDP on defense, depending on the situation, and built up a nuclear arsenal of unimaginable destructive power. It fought two regional wars in Korea and Vietnam at the cost of more than eighty-five thousand American lives. Overall, America engaged in such consistent brinkmanship with the Soviet Union that the "Doomsday Clock" of the *Bulletin of Atomic Scientists* was kept at between five minutes and one minute to twelve for almost the entire period.

That bipolar rivalry is now a relic of the past, and while an issue such as the war on terrorism seems to loom quite large, it does not even begin to compare with the tensions and gravity of the nuclear confrontation between the United States and the Soviet Union in the second half of the last century. The United States, indeed the entire world, is now unfettered by an overarching strategic rivalry in which everyone must participate, take sides, and make sacrifices to sustain.

THE AMERICAN MOMENT OF CHOICE   So great is the power of the United States that it operates in what policy analysts Stephen Brooks and William Wohlforth call "the realm of choice rather than necessity"[3] and it does so to a greater degree than any other power in modern history. The unipolar moment is a moment of choice for America. It allows Americans and the international community the time to reflect on the implications of imperial power and its proper utility in a globalizing world.

The temptation for America is to exult in its power and engage in a unilateralism of narrow self-interest. But the question must be asked: If America is already on top, what utility is there in alienating friends and allies for further short-term gains? Surely, this does not aggregate more power and only ends up reducing the pool of goodwill from which America will inevitably want to draw down the road, a lesson it learned during the run-up to and invasion of Iraq. Thus both policy elites and citizens must ponder the question: Are there other options that both enhance U.S. power and contribute to the world as a whole?

It is this freedom to choose between self-interest and the common good that is the most fundamental challenge to the empire America has become. It can no longer think and act in ways motivated purely by self-interest without damaging that self-interest. It must combine its self-interest with the interests of the whole because it now dominates the whole. Because its dominion is planetary, its interests must be planetary. This is a precious but very fragile moment, one that has never occurred before in the long journey of humankind, one that must be used for both deep reflection and imaginative action.

THE CRISIS OF THE NATION-STATE SYSTEM   The tiny fly in the ointment takes shape with the notion that America may not be up to the task, a concern raised by Henry Kissinger in his book *Does America Need a Foreign Policy?* He agrees that the United States has reached its apogee moment, opening his book with the observation: "At the dawn of the new millennium, the United States is enjoying a preeminence unrivaled by even the greatest empires of the past."[4]

But this does not make the situation straightforward, he says. On the one hand, the United States is sufficiently able to do what it wants internationally. On the other hand, American prescriptions for the rest of the world are often the result of domestic concerns or a reiteration of Cold War rhetoric that has little relevance to current international conditions. "The result is that the country's preeminence is coupled with the serious potential of becoming irrelevant to many of the currents affecting and ultimately transforming the global order."[5]

At the apogee moment of global dominion, says Kissinger, the United States finds itself in an ironic position: "In the face of perhaps the most profound and widespread upheavals the world has ever seen, it has failed to develop concepts relevant to the emerging realities." Instead of looking ahead and setting an ambitious international agenda, American leaders have rested on the laurels of winning the Cold War and have confused economic dynamism with strategic advantage, making them "less sensitive to the political, cultural, and spiritual impact of the vast transformations brought about by American technology."[6]

This malaise, says Kissinger, has given rise to two competing but equally misleading worldviews about recent history and America's destiny. On the one hand, American liberals tend to view the role of the United States in the world as the ultimate arbiter of all social ills, if only it would reprioritize its foreign policy along humanitarian lines and spend enough money. Many liberals act "as if the United States has the appropriate democratic solution for every other society regardless of cultural and historical differences. For this school of thought, foreign policy equates with social policy."[7]

On the other hand, American conservatives tend to view the collapse of the Soviet Union as the singular achievement of the assertiveness of President Reagan in the 1980s rather than of the combined efforts of bipartisan efforts over nine administrations spanning nearly fifty years. For many conservatives, "the solution to the world's ills is American hegemony—the imposition of American solutions on the world's trouble spots by the unabashed affirmation of its preeminence."[8]

Neither approach on its own, says Kissinger, can provide sound strategic guidance for future action. Even conjoined, they miss the mark because neither is based on a realistic analysis of the world in transition. The real issue, he says, is how the United States will address "the inevitable transformation of the international order resulting from changes in the internal structure of many of its key participants, and from the democratization of politics, the globalization of economies, and the instantaneousness of communications."[9]

This confluence of forces is eroding the basis of the nation-state itself, of which the United States is but one, even if preeminent. "The Westphalian order is in systemic crisis,"[10] says Kissinger, which means that the very predicate upon which U.S. power rests is unstable. At the apogee point of national power, the United States finds itself in a situation that is abrading the very basis of that power. Indeed, it is the breakdown of the nation-state system that is simultaneously exaggerating American power even as it undermines it.

Kissinger reminds us that the term *international relations* is quite new, originating in the late eighteenth century and being spread around the world by European colonialism. The current nation-state system emerged out of the ashes of the Thirty Years' War that consumed 30 percent of the population of central Europe in the early seventeenth century. Out of this carnage, the modern system of nation-states emerged, as codified in 1648 by the Treaty of Westphalia. The principles of Westphalia have shaped international affairs to the present day. The basic doctrine is that of *national sovereignty*—the notion that national borders should be respected and that states should not interfere in the domestic affairs of other states. A corollary principle is that of a balance of power between states, the notion that no state should be allowed to become too dominant.

The issues challenging the nation-state and the current notion of national sovereignty are detailed by Jean-François Rischard, Vice President for Europe at the World Bank, in his book *High Noon*. He lists twenty global challenges currently being exacerbated by the limitations of the nation-state system. First, there are the issues having to do with the health of the planet itself: global warming, biodiversity and ecosystem losses, fisheries depletion, deforestation, water shortages and pollution, and maritime safety and pollution.

Then there are the critical human issues requiring urgent attention: ameliorating poverty, keeping the peace and preventing conflicts, providing primary school education, fighting infectious diseases such as HIV AIDS as well as illegal drugs, overcoming the digital divide, and coping with natural disasters such as hurricanes, earthquakes, and tornadoes. Finally, there are the global commerce issues: international taxation, biotechnology rules, the global financial architecture, trade, investment, and competition rules, intellectual property rights, e-commerce regulations, and international labor and migration rules.

Rischard makes a point very similar to Kissinger's. "The complexity of many global issues and their lack of boundaries do not sit well with the territorial and hierarchical institutions that are supposed to solve them: the nation-states."[11] The nation-states themselves have acknowledged this and set up a variety of mechanisms to help them deal with the issues: treaties and conventions; intergovernmental conferences such as U.N. conferences, the G8, and the G77; and an array of over forty international institutions ranging from the World Bank to the World Trade Organization. But none of the attempts on the part of the nation-states to solve these problems is working effectively. Every single one of the twenty global problems identified by Rischard have become chronic, and many have become acute.

The common characteristic of all the treaties, conferences, and institutions convened or established by governments to solve these problems is that they are limited exclusively to representatives of nation-states. Because of the complexities of relationships between the nations and the complexities of domestic politics inside each nation, the pace of decision making is glacial. Furthermore, the decisions made reflect *avoidance* of the issues more than actually making the compromises necessary to *solve* the issues. What emerges in reality is rhetoric rather than decisions, postponement rather than action. Thus the U.N. conferences and the G8 summits resound with pronouncements, but when all is said and done, much is said and little is done. Meanwhile, the problems worsen and the suffering of the people and planet intensifies.

THE PROMISE AND CHALLENGE OF GLOBALIZATION   The problems listed by Rischard are only part of the overall challenge to the United States and the nation-state system. Taken cumulatively, the integration of the world as a whole, particularly in terms of economic globalization and the mythic qualities of "free market" capitalism, represents a veritable "empire" in its own right. Globalization is pervasive and overwhelming, subsuming the entire global polity under its control. In some ways, globalization represents the "rise in the machines."

No nation on earth has been able to resist the compelling magnetism of globalization. Few have been able to escape the "structural adjustments" and "conditionalities" of the World Bank, the International Monetary Fund, or the arbitrations of the World Trade Organization, those international financial institutions that, however inadequate, still determine what economic globalization means, what the rules are, and who is rewarded for submission and punished for infractions. Such is the power of globalization that within our lifetime we are likely to see the integration, even if unevenly, of all national economies in the world into a single global, free market system.

At one level, this is the goal of U.S. policy and the intention of the "Washington consensus": to break down national barriers to trade, end protectionism, expand free markets and free trade zones, and allow capital to flow anywhere with minimal restraint or regulation. The United States is in fact the driving force behind these economic policies and draws the most benefit from their application.

At a deeper level, however, globalization marks the first time an empire like America has faced a supraordinant force that is not geographically rooted and that is not national in scope. Before globalization, the world, historically considered, was flat. Empires rose and fell, dealing with other emergent or declining states that were physically defined and geographically bounded. Globalization is the Copernican revolution of our day. It is making the world truly round because it is bringing all of humanity into a single ecosystem of embedded, overlapping networks. Borders, boundaries, delineations, and walls of any kind are slowly giving way to the compelling force of integration and interdependence.

Herein lies the long-term challenge for the American imperium, which at present is using globalization so skillfully to further American interests. Economic globalization is now the servant of the United States, but in time, it will become the master. When this occurs, negligence on the part of the United States in keeping its own house in order and its fiscal and economic policies on a sound footing—extremely difficult to do while at the same time maintaining its global interests—could bring it to its knees faster than it can imagine. A meltdown of markets and economies like that in Southeast Asia in 1997 could happen, certainly in a different way but with the same destructive effect, in the United States.

It is thus important to understand that while economic globalization may be the wave of the future, it also has a significant riptide. Free market economics and free trade zones, while indispensable for wealth generation, are also creating serious deleterious effects on the environment and on society. In free trade zones and under the current rules of the WTO, capital can now move almost anywhere at anytime. People cannot. The ability of capital to move also undermines the ability of the state to exercise control over its economy. The globalization of capital markets after World War II undermined the welfare states of the industrial nations because the people who required a safety net could not leave the country, but the capital these states needed to tax could.

This state of affairs is not an accidental side effect of the globalization process but a direct result of government policies, beginning with the Reagan administration in 1980 and carried forward by every American administration since then. It has been a policy of what George Soros in his book *On Globalization* calls *market fundamentalism,* which holds that the allocation of resources is best left to market forces and that any interference in the market reduces economic efficiency. Gripped by this conviction, the United States has relentlessly pushed forward the proposition that an unfettered free market will solve virtually any problem a nation or society has.

The problem with this worldview, says Soros, is that "markets are amoral: they allow people to act in accordance with their interests, and they impose some rules on how those interests are expressed, but they pass no moral judgment on the interests themselves."[12] Markets are designed for the free exchange of goods and services among those participating in the markets. This is why they are so efficient. By leaving out morality, markets let individuals pursue their self-interest unimpeded.

While this allows for remarkable wealth generation, it does not produce justice or ensure equity. Markets are not capable, on their own, of taking care of social needs such as law and order, environmental regulations, worker health and safety norms, or care for the vulnerable. Markets alone cannot fulfill the demands of a good society. These "public goods" are only provided for by a political process through which citizens deliberate and agree on moral norms and social priorities.

The United States has done one of the best jobs of any nation in the world in placing the private pursuit of wealth into a framework of regulations that prevents monopolistic control, protects workers, safeguards the environment, and ensures social justice for its citizens. This is one of the reasons it is so strong. Unfortunately, the United States has been the leader in insisting that economic globalization abroad gives primacy to trade and investment to the denigration of most of the social regulations the United States insists upon at home.

Soros points to three results of these *neoliberal* policies: the erosion of social safety nets not only throughout the global south but increasingly in the industrial north; a misallocation of resources between private gain and public goods, so that environmental protection and other social norms are eroded; and increasing instability in financial markets, leading to a global financial system that is susceptible to meltdowns and crises, such as the collapse of the East Asian markets in 1997 and the bankruptcy of Argentina in 2002.

The current emphasis on market liberalization to the diminution of social equity frameworks tolerates a world of staggering poverty and deprivation. The statistics on human suffering are becoming increasingly well-known, even if they remain unaddressed:

• Forty-seven percent of the world's population lives on less than $2 per day.

- Forty percent does not have access to electricity.
- Thirty-three percent of all the children in the world under five suffer from malnutrition, with roughly thirty thousand dying every twenty-four hours of preventable diseases.
- Twenty-five percent of all adults worldwide are illiterate.
- Twenty percent of the world's population does not have access to health care.

These statistics represent billions of people who live in the developing world and in nations so crippled by foreign debt, corruption, and ethnic strife that many are essentially ungovernable and many others exist on the verge of bankruptcy and collapse. Billions of people are living on the margins of life, flooding into cities, desperately looking for work and access to the material affluence they see on American television, whether in the mountains of Nepal, the deserts of Arabia, the floodplains of Amazonia, or the steppes of Siberia. Most of the world is desperately poor, and yet the whole world watches the "good life" unfold in American movies and television.

Shows like *Bay Watch* and *Dynasty* depict a life of sensuality and sumptuousness that many of the viewing audiences in the global south assume is "normal life" in the U.S.A., making it seem like the best of times for anyone living there. Indeed, the American people, representing roughly 4 percent of the human population, do in fact consume roughly 25 percent of the world's resources. Europe is not far behind, while much of Latin America, Africa, and South Asia are essentially destitute.

To take one small example: one person in the United States uses 680 liters of water per day, in France about 200, in Kenya only 4. These differences are roughly the same in the amount of food eaten, electricity used, garbage produced, and energy consumed. America's imperial footprint is huge, and made to appear even more dominant by the pervasive power of American media.

The growing disparity between the rich and the poor, accentuated by the current policies governing economic globalization, is replicated in the growing disparity between the sophistication of our consumer goods and the price the planet is forced to pay to provide such a lavish lifestyle for the small minority of wealthy consumers. The use of fossil fuels, for example, has increased by

500 percent in the past fifty years, meaning that the world uses in six weeks what in 1950 it took one year to consume. One of the results of this is carbon emissions. The world's atmosphere is capable of absorbing roughly one-third of the carbonic gases that are produced each year. The other two-thirds are not absorbed and contribute to the greenhouse effect that is leading to global warming. In terms of its imperial footprint, the United States produces about ten times as much carbon emissions per capita than does China, and twenty times more than India.

One of the effects of global warming is climate change, leading to increases in natural disasters such as floods, droughts, storms, and fires as well as the spread of pestilence and disease. Epidemics like SARS, which broke out without warning in 2003, will only increase in frequency and virulence as global warming continues. Meanwhile, the U.S. government walked away from the Kyoto protocol with a casual disregard. Understandably, this was deemed extraordinary and arrogant by the rest of the international community.

It is this kind of dereliction of leadership that will lead to America's demise far more quickly than any terrorist threat within its gates, and these will become only more frequent and acute.

WARRIOR POLITICS   Emerging from the social desperation embodied in the above statistics is what journalist Robert Kaplan calls *warrior politics*. Warfare in the future will be much more along the lines of the September 11 attacks than massive armies confronting one another along national borders. The enemies of the United States will not, in the short term, be other nations. They will be small rebel groups like al-Qaeda, using technologies and tactics against which it will have few viable defenses simply because they are so small and the United States so muscle-bound.

A direct consequence of globalization is the democratization of power. Globalization affects everyone everywhere, and so it empowers small players in ways that were unthinkable only a few years ago. Currency traders can bring down developing nations in a few days, something that would have been inconceivable before the globalization of currency markets but is now eminently possible because of their interconnections and the absence of any international regulatory framework to modulate the market's "invisible hand."

Similarly, before the Internet and the advances in banking communications and the worldwide armaments market, a Saudi businessman like Osama bin Laden would not have been able to mobilize a small army, train it in an array of countries, and declare war against the United States. But now people with cell phones and access to explosives can go almost anywhere and destroy almost anything if they have the right means and the determination, and especially if they are willing to die to ensure the success of the mission. Networks are now as powerful as nations.

Globalization means the privatization of markets. It also means the democratization of violence. Thus the power of the United States, at one level invincible, is at a deeper level extremely vulnerable to small players and unnoticed events. The story of David and Goliath is perhaps as likely today as it was unlikely when it was written. The lesson here is that the United States should never confuse invincibility with invulnerability.

Over the short term, terrorism, with globalization, will be the wave of the future. Indeed, terrorism against America will only intensify because America is attaining imperial status at the worst of times for many around the world, and many of the deprived blame America for their plight. To the degree to which America continues to ignore them and insist on the implementation of free trade zones around the world without regulations that ensure social equity or environmental protection, it will face a rising tide of discontent and violence.

LEADING IN A TIME OF CRISIS   Thus, although it is indisputably true that America has attained world dominion, it is equally true, if less recognized, that the globalizing world in which America reigns supreme is very fragile. America has reached its supremacy precisely at the moment when the challenges confronting the international community are reaching multiple crisis points, spilling across borders, eroding the foundations of the international system, and challenging the entire international community, especially the United States, to respond collectively and dramatically.

What must be stressed about these global challenges is that they are all occurring simultaneously and with interacting and mutually generative complexity. They appear separate and distinct but in fact are interconnected and interactive. They form a single ecology of relatedness. Environmental problems have social and financial effects, and social problems have political and economic repercussions in an interlocking complexity that defies simple analysis or local solutions. We are witnessing the integration of the world to a large degree because the crises confronting the world are integrating and forcing us to develop coping mechanisms that are as global as our problems are.

In such a situation, American strength is simultaneously more magnified and increasingly vulnerable. Its power is being exercised in a global system that could collapse at any moment from a range of social, political, and environmental pressures so intricately interconnected that it is difficult to discern where one ends and another begins. The United States must carefully calibrate the effects of large actions and small nuances, knowing that each has a ripple effect throughout the entire global system and can cause serious damage to the American economy and way of life. The "butterfly effect" of chaos theory—whereby the flutter of a butterfly's wings over China can eventually cause a storm in Europe—is now a fact of life in every domain.

The United States must act and lead inside the paradoxical reality that, as powerful as it is, most of the events affecting the world and causing destabilization are actually outside of state control. It must also act and lead in a global context characterized by the deeply complex intermixture of culture and belief with poverty and alienation. Where there is little hope, power has little effect. One of the deepest truths of history is that people in despair will act out of their powerlessness in ways that confound the powerful. This is the strength behind terrorism.

It is America's current lack of strategic imagination and proactive leadership on these issues that is the most fundamental contributor to the world's inability to solve its global challenges. That in the aftermath of September 11 it is acting unilaterally and aggressively, pursuing the narrowest self-interest, only makes the situation worse. September 11 may go down as one of the most tragic events in modern history not only because of the thousands of deaths it caused but also because it so seriously distorted American perceptions about itself and the world. It has knocked America down into a dank and dangerous cul de sac, making it susceptible to apocalyptic visions of darkness rather than motivating it toward high visions of human possibility.

More than at any time since the end of the Second World War, the United States needs to rise to a higher vision and provide leadership in determining what a post-Westphalian order will look like. In that context, it must actively lead the global community to solve specific problems. But in many cases—global warming being a prime example—the United States actually blocks attempts by the international community to solve the global problems at hand.

The gravity of this situation can be seen in the fact that when political structures and governing institutions get out of touch with the people they govern, social unrest is generated. When the gap becomes sufficiently wide, revolt and revolution ensue until a new equilibrium is established between the government and the governed. The fact that crises press down upon the world community from all sides, combined with the systemic failure of the governing institutions to cope, means that we are not only in a time of global crisis, we are in a time of potential revolution.

At the core of the challenge ahead is the need to rework existing institutions and establish the new mechanisms and institutions necessary for the effective management of the global system. The current system of nation-states needs to be replaced by a transnational system of integrated global management. This will necessitate the development of network democracy and global issue networks, to be discussed in more detail in the last chapter, which enhance the power of governments by bringing the expertise of the civil society and business sectors to bear on specific issues of concern.

The United States, as world leader, should exercise both the imagination and the decisiveness to direct the way. This is what it means to be a transitional empire. The United States must use its national sovereignty to establish an effective and democratic global system. Otherwise, the international system will continue to degenerate into increasing chaos and disorder, leading to what policymakers call "catastrophic futures" and "extreme events." U.S. dominance, which today seems so overwhelming, could then easily be overwhelmed by the chaos it brings about by its failure to lead.

3
America's Journey to Empire

RATHER THAN DEAL WITH THE CRISIS of the nation-state system or seriously take on any of the global challenges crippling human affairs, except for HIV AIDS, to which it has made a small gesture, the Bush administration is doing what empires universally have done at their moment of preeminence: further consolidate military control. This is a natural, indeed necessary, action for any empire to accomplish; otherwise, its dominion is not secure. Military might seeks to make durable what is inherently unstable. But under current circumstances, further consolidating military supremacy in an increasingly unsustainable international system might turn out to be more like arranging deck chairs on the *Titanic*.

The Bush administration is building on the work of previous administrations to consolidate what the Pentagon calls *full spectrum dominance*. The cornerstone of this policy is "the ability of U.S. forces, operating either unilaterally or in combination with multinational and interagency partners, to defeat any adversary and control any situation across the full range of military operations." This implies that "U.S. forces are able to conduct prompt, sustained, and synchronized operations with combinations of forces tailored to specific situations, and with access and freedom to operate in all domains—space, sea, land, air, and information."[1]

49

Full spectrum dominance enables the U.S. military to fulfill its primary purpose—victory at war.

THE NEW AMERICAN INTERNATIONALISM OF GEORGE W.
BUSH   A refinement of the Bush military policies was contained in a comprehensive policy report released on September 20, 2002 by the White House titled "The National Security Strategy of the United States." The first major point raised is an exultation of America winning the Cold War: "The great struggles of the twentieth century between liberty and totalitarianism ended with a decisive victory for the forces of freedom—and a single sustainable model for national success: freedom, democracy, and free enterprise. . . . These values of freedom are right and true for every person, in every society—and the duty of protecting these values against their enemies is the common calling of freedom-loving people across the globe and across the ages." The United States has been and will continue to be the leader of this great enterprise, says the report. It will use its strength to "create a balance of power that favors human freedom."[2]

The report does not mention any systemic challenges to the international system resulting from the democratization of politics, the globalization of economies, or the spread of instantaneous communication. Nor does it note any of the twenty global challenges listed by Jean-François Rischard, with the exception of HIV AIDS and poverty. The report simply states that the task of defending the nation and the principles of freedom is the most fundamental responsibility of the U.S. government: "Enemies in the past needed great armies and great industrial capabilities to endanger America. Now, shadowy networks of individuals can bring great chaos and suffering to our shores for less than it costs to purchase a single tank. Terrorists are organized to penetrate open societies and to turn the power of modern technologies against us."[3]

The lesson of 9/11 was that "weak states, like Afghanistan, can pose as great a danger to our national interests as strong states. Poverty does not make poor people into terrorists and murderers. Yet poverty, weak institutions, and corruption can make weak states vulnerable to terrorist networks and drug cartels within their borders." The gravest threat that the United States now faces lies at "the crossroads of radicalism and technology."[4]

In the face of this new threat, new measures are needed. "In the Cold War, especially following the Cuban missile crisis, we faced a generally status quo, risk-averse adversary. Deterrence was an effective defense. But deterrence based only upon the threat of retaliation is less likely to work against leaders of rogue states more willing to take risks, gambling with the lives of their people and the wealth of their nations." Terrorist networks are even more difficult to counter. The only credible, indeed moral, defense against those for whom deterrence has no power is what the report calls "proactive counterproliferation," meaning that the United States "must deter and defend against the threat before it is unleashed."[5]

Noting the willingness of terrorists to use any method to achieve any aim, the report states that "the United States can no longer solely rely on a reactive posture as we have in the past. The inability to deter a potential attacker, the immediacy of today's threats, and the magnitude of potential harm that could be caused by our adversaries' choice of weapons, do not permit that option. We cannot let our enemies strike first." The United States will, if necessary, act "preemptively."[6]

More broadly, the report states that the United States will continue to protect its military superiority around the world. "The President has no intention of allowing any foreign power to catch up with the huge lead the United States has opened since the fall of the Soviet Union more than a decade ago." U.S. military forces "will be strong enough to dissuade potential adversaries from pursuing a military buildup in hopes of surpassing, or equaling, the power of the United States."[7]

This strategy for a "new American internationalism" articulates for the first time since the end of the Cold War that the doctrine of deterrence is being superceded by the doctrine of preemptive strike. For the first time since the founding of the republic, the United States is the unrivaled military power in the world and will take any steps necessary to keep it that way. The Bush administration has declared that it will work collectively if it can, and unilaterally if it must, to protect American interests and that America has reached the point of strength where it will not share its power or allow it to be challenged by anyone anywhere.

A key component of this new strategic posture has been the political strategy of withdrawing the United States from various multilateral treaty obligations that circumscribe the ability of the United States to act unimpeded in world affairs. The Bush administration has withdrawn from more international treaties than any administration in American history. Among others, it withdrew from the 1972 Antiballistic Missile Treaty and the Kyoto Protocol on Global Warming. It rejected the enforcement protocol of the 1972 Biological Weapons Convention and opposed the International Criminal Court (also opposed by previous administrations). It voiced opposition to the 1963 Comprehensive Nuclear Test Ban Treaty and scuttled the U.N. negotiations on small arms.

In 2002, the Bush administration forced out Robert Watson, chairman of the Intergovernmental Panel on Climate Change; ousted Jose Bustani, director-general of the 145-nation Organization for the Prohibition of Chemical Weapons; and lobbied against the reappointment of Mary Robinson as U.N. High Commissioner for Human Rights. In 2003, it brushed aside objections from the U.N. Security Council and invaded Iraq. The objective of all these actions? To create room to maneuver, to allow for ad hoc alliances when deemed necessary, to weaken international bodies or at least make their leadership more compliant with U.S. interests, and to further consolidate military control. This is the classic behavior of empire.

The only treaty obligations the Bush administration actively supports are the trade agreements that enhance the economic power of the United States. At the same time, the Bush administration feels free to impose protectionist tariffs, whether to protect its farmers or its steel industry. In character with an imperial power, the Bush administration is exercising its power unilaterally and in the spirit of U.S. "exceptionalism."

Two important points need to be made about Bush's strategy and actions. First, they are the outcome of serious thinking and planning by his closest advisers, developed long before his presidency began. Second, they are both the culmination and the logical extension of more than two hundred years of American foreign policy. September 11 may have provided the occasion, but it was not the reason for the "new American internationalism" of the Bush presidency. The reasons lie deep in America's past.

FROM BUSH I TO BUSH II   The immediate origins of the current Bush policies begin in the administration of his father, principally with Dick Cheney, who was then secretary of defense. After the fall of the Berlin Wall in 1989, Cheney convened a small group of advisers to think through American foreign policy after the Cold War at a grand strategic level. Among the group was Paul Wolfowitz, currently deputy secretary of defense; Lewis Libby, currently Cheney's chief of staff; and Eric Edelman, currently a senior foreign policy adviser to Cheney. These were all committed *neoconservatives,* who considered themselves to be tough-minded but bigger thinking than most of their other colleagues in Washington.

At the same time, Colin Powell, then chairman of the Joint Chiefs of Staff, mounted a similar effort to reimagine American post–Cold War foreign and defense policy, drawing into his circle a more moderate group of thinkers who were multilateralist in their orientation and diplomatic in their tactical considerations.

A date was set—May 21, 1990—on which each team would brief Cheney, who would then brief George Bush, Sr., after which the president would make a major foreign policy address detailing the grand new strategy. Both teams worked for several months on the "5/21 brief" with the sense that the shape of America's post–Cold War strategy was as stake. On the appointed day, both Wolfowitz and Powell showed up. Wolfowitz went first, but his briefing lasted far beyond the allotted one hour, so Powell's presentation was rescheduled for a few weeks later. Cheney then briefed the president, using material drawn primarily from Wolfowitz.

On August 2, 1990, the president delivered his address, and in very diplomatic and general terms, articulated the position that the United States was aware of the dramatically altered geostrategic landscape and would proceed accordingly. Unfortunately, this was also the day Saddam Hussein invaded Kuwait. The rest, as they say, is history.

Despite the pressures of the Gulf War, the Cheney-Wolfowitz team kept working. For them, any rethinking of American strategy must take into consideration the central reality of American military preeminence. Accordingly, the Defense Planning Guidance that Wolfowitz drafted in the wake of the Persian Gulf War stated that U.S. strategy should focus on "convincing potential competitors that they need not aspire to a greater role or pursue a more aggressive posture to protect their legitimate interests." Properly conceived, American policies should "sufficiently account for the interests of the advanced industrial nations to discourage them from challenging our leadership or seeking to overturn the established political and economic order." However, it was also incumbent upon the United States to "maintain the mechanisms for deterring potential competitors from even aspiring to a larger regional or global role."[8]

On March 8, 1992, the *New York Times* leaked a copy of what Wolfowitz was circulating in the executive branch and reported that the Pentagon envisioned a future in which the United States would take any steps necessary to prevent any other nation or group of nations from seriously challenging U.S. power. Cheney's team sought to ameliorate the controversy by releasing a counterleaked document that was much softer and more diplomatic in tone.

When it became clear that Bush was going to lose to Bill Clinton, the Wolfowitz team formally codified their thinking into a document entitled "Defense Strategy for the 1990s," which was released in January 1991, just as the Clinton administration was coming in. It was an even more diplomatic rendition of the original thinking, but subtly emphasized that the United States needed to preserve the "strategic depth won at such great pains" during the Cold War while working within a multilateral international framework.

A more forthright version of these ideas came out in 1995 in *From Containment to Global Leadership?*, a small book by Zalmay

Khalizad, who joined Cheney's team in 1991 and served as President Bush's special envoy to the Iraqi opposition groups before the invasion in 2003. In it Khalizad stated:

> As the victor of the Cold War, the United States can choose among several strategic visions and grand strategies. It could abandon global leadership and turn inward. It could seek to give up leadership gradually by reducing its global role and encouraging the emergence of an old-fashioned balance-of-power structure with spheres of influence. Or the central strategic objective for the United States could be to consolidate its global leadership and preclude the rise of a global rival.[9]

Khalizad argued that it is crucial for the United States to develop a "grand design" that will provide the strategic direction it needs to use its overwhelming power effectively. The most fundamental component of this design is that "the United States must resolve to maintain its position of global leadership and preclude the rise of another global rival for the indefinite future. It is an opportunity the nation may never see again."[10] Khalizad argued that the United States must be prepared to use force against any nation or group of nations seeking to compete in this domain.

Having first secured total military dominance, the United States must then maintain and incrementally extend the "zone of democracy" and the "zone of peace" worldwide. It must prevent hostile powers from taking over critical regions and deal firmly with any renewed Russian or Chinese expansionism. It must maintain U.S. economic strength, and further consolidate free market economies worldwide and judiciously use military force while avoiding overextension. It must nurture and maintain the support of the American public for this new American role. Above all, the United States must use its military power to ensure that no other power can seriously challenge its military superiority or political dominance.

This neoconservative vision is intensely nationalistic with a fundamental emphasis on the use of America's military superiority to effectuate U.S. policy. It is essentially Jacksonian, believing that military power is the solution to political conflict and that the United States should view the world only in terms of its national interest. The United Nations in this view should be marginalized, and the United States should withdraw from any agreements or treaties that encumber its ability to act unilaterally.

As this view developed during the 1990s, the neoconservatives came to believe that the greatest use of American military power would be to eliminate what they considered to be rogue states: Iran, Iraq, and North Korea in particular (the Axis of Evil), but also Pakistan and Syria. Iraq and North Korea would require military action; Syria and Iran could be destabilized through covert operations and economic and political pressure; and Pakistan could simply be absorbed in the U.S. military and intelligence sphere of influence. If this could be achieved, they believed, the world would be much safer for the expanding zones of democracy and peace.

The Cheney team has been developing and implementing this strategic thinking since the inauguration of George W. Bush as president. For them, the attack of September 11 was the equivalent to Pearl Harbor. It afforded the United States the opportunity to legitimate a highly aggressive strategy of conquest that would have been inconceivable during the Hamiltonian era of President Clinton. Its most fundamental tenet is that the United States must use its moment of preeminence to consolidate global military dominance and secure for itself unthreatened military primacy over the world. Indeed, Bush's advisers project that the United States can maintain complete global dominance, based on military supremacy, for at least the next fifty to seventy-five years.

AMERICA'S ORIGINS IN THE LIGHT   Beneath the thinking and planning of the Bush administration is the historical trajectory of American foreign policy itself. It is often taken as a virtual truism, particularly in Europe, that Americans know little about foreign policy or the rest of the world and that American diplomats generally bumble along, vacillating between naive idealism and crass self-interest. Americans are almost universally considered to be politically naive.

There is certainly a tension in American foreign policy between the democratic ideals on which the country was founded and the cynical realities of power politics. But the fact is that the United States has had the most successful foreign policy of any nation in the modern world. This is why the United States emerged as the undisputed power in the world when the Soviet Union collapsed in 1991. The power that the United States possesses today is the result of more than two centuries of highly aggressive and generally successful foreign policy strategies. It is within this deeper context that the national security strategy of the Bush administration and the larger issue of U.S. global dominance must be understood.

What is crucial in understanding American power is that it was generated out of a unique and profound commitment to light. The United States was founded by political mystics steeped in the writings of the ancient mystery religions and in the esoteric teachings of Judaism and Christianity. They were conscious that what they were doing was of deep spiritual as well as historical significance. This is what has always given the United States its unique destiny of light and power.

Of particular importance to the thinking and politics of the founding fathers was the work of Francis Bacon, who, in some ways, was the spiritual godfather of the American republic. Bacon left a legacy of achievement unrivaled in his generation. He was a writer who some scholars believe authored several of the works attributed to Shakespeare, a scientist who helped shape the basis of modern science with his theories of an empirical scientific method, and, hidden from public view, one of the great secular mystics of his age. He was friend and counselor to Queen Elizabeth I and King James I, serving as attorney general and lord chancellor. He was also a friend of the explorer Sir Walter Raleigh.

Raleigh had tried unsuccessfully to found a colony in what is now North Carolina. Although he failed in doing that, he brought back and introduced to England potatoes and tobacco, at the same time igniting Europe's imagination with the possibilities of the New World. It was Bacon who penned the first popular expression of these possibilities in a curious little manuscript titled *New Atlantis,* which he wrote in 1624 but which was published posthumously in 1627.[11]

Inspired by Raleigh's tales of a vast land of untapped resources and scarcely peopled, *New Atlantis* told the story of a group of sailors who venture forth from Peru and are blown off-course northward. There they find a previously undiscovered island called Bensalem, which is governed by the House of Salomon.

The House of Salomon was undeniably wise. In its exploration of the "true nature of things," it would send out an expedition every twelve years to trade "not for gold, silver, or jewels; nor for silk, nor for spices; nor any other commodity of matter; but only for God's first creature, which was Light: to have Light of the growth of all parts of the world."[12] The House of Salomon had what it called "Perspective Houses" where "all multiplications of light" were demonstrated.

This focus on light provided the House of Salomon with the capacity for good governance. "Happy are the people of Bensalem," the governor in the book declares. "There is not under heaven so chaste a nation as this of Bensalem; nor so free from all pollution or foulness. It is a virgin of the world."[13] The people were happy because within constraints they were free and within limits their needs were met.

Their government was benign, their science enabled them to attain a state of material affluence, and they were motivated by the mysteries of light. Christianity also helped the Bensalemites maintain moral balance and keep their baser impulses in check. All this allowed for an ambiguous happiness as the complexities of their nature interfaced with their dreams of perfection.

Yet Bensalem had a secret past. As the title of the book suggests, Bensalem was the site of the ancient empire of Atlantis, which Bacon described as "all poetical and fabulous," with a magnificent city with a temple and palace, navigable rivers, and a mountain that was a "ladder to heaven." It became mighty in armaments, commerce, and riches—so mighty that the king commanded two expeditions to sail forth, one east across the Atlantic and one west across the Pacific, and circumnavigate and conquer the world on behalf of his empire. But these proud exploits came to naught, and none of the sailors returned. Then "Divine Revenge" overtook Atlantis, and it was destroyed in a great flood, leaving only a remnant of survivors.

What is extraordinary to note here is that it was a vision of Atlantis that provided the spark that became the United States of America. At its earliest point of origin, at the very moment of its inception as a possibility, what was to become the United States was imprinted with a vision of the original mythopoetic civilization and empire. This vision framed America's destiny path as a nation, and in Bacon's mind, destined it to the same global greatness but also to the same total destruction if its power was corrupted by arrogance. This vision was what was bestowed upon America by the greatest secular mystic of his age: a vision of light against the backdrop of extraordinary power and spectacular doom.

It is said that the Atlanteans used crystals with the same proficiency that we today have learned to use the power of the atom, as a source of almost total power. It is also said that the Atlanteans perfected the arts of cloning and bioengineering, designing the centaurs, creatures that were half human and half horse, as well as other composite beings such as the unicorn and griffin described in ancient mythology.

Then something very dark happened. At the moment when the kings of Atlantis embarked on the campaign to conquer the world, the crystals they possessed were somehow ignited and shattered the Atlantean world like a pure sound hitting a glass. This caused volcanic eruptions and a great tsunami to rise up from far out in the Atlantic ocean and wash the entire civilization away into the myths of legend and time.

Plato wrote of the greatness, arrogance, and demise of Atlantis in the *Critias*, although the account was not completed because *Critias* was never finished. He made another reference to its destruction in the *Timaeus*. Other Greek and Roman thinkers, as well as church fathers such as Origen, wrote about the allegorical meaning of what was then believed to be the world's first civilization. Then for two thousand years Atlantis faded from conscious memory, kept alive only in the mystical esoteric traditions, until Francis Bacon called up its grandeur in describing the possibilities of the New World.

In this sense, and worth reflecting upon, the United States is Atlantis *recidivus*. It is the most modern expression of the most ancient quest of humankind: the quest for absolute power through complete knowledge, tempted by hubris, and caught in the choice between domination or stewardship.

In the land that Bacon depicted, a mythical descendant of the fallen Atlantis, the leadership was preoccupied with how to govern effectively so that its people could attain happiness. A pioneer in the scientific method, Bacon was thus the first philosopher to suggest that society could be improved through science. Previous utopias, going all the way back to the one described in Plato's *Republic*, were achieved through social legislation, religious reforms, or the spread of knowledge. But in *New Atlantis,* Bacon joined science with power. He understood that utopia could come about not by denying the complexity of human nature but by exploiting it.

Bacon understood that since human nature cannot be changed, the idea of human perfection, however compelling, in the end cannot endure. He believed that the best that humans can do is assume the vagaries of the human heart and build good government to check its impulses while seeking to satisfy the material needs of the people. Most importantly, we should focus on light rather than darkness as the most fundamental organizing principle of society.

New Atlantis had a profound effect on Europeans of the time because it shifted the notion of utopia away from being a separate reality in a never-never land, where people were miraculously good, to something grounded in human complexity that was made possible through good governance and practical technology. Bacon's utopia, if imperfect, was attainable. In this sense, he described the first realistic utopia. It appealed to his contemporaries because he created a vision of a better world, not by changing the human heart but by transforming nature itself for human benefit. He redefined perfection as not about being a place of moral purity but as being a possibility of freedom and material satisfaction.

While challenging the reader to take seriously the ambiguities of the human psyche, *New Atlantis* evokes a deep admiration for the intelligence and ingenuity that could produce the scientific wonders necessary to alleviate want. Bacon invoked the lost civilization of Atlantis to underscore that Paradise was and can be lost; but he reframed that ancient myth and cautionary tale within the possibility of a *new* Atlantis that could be created in the New World Europeans had just discovered. Paradise could be rebuilt in the "virgin country" of America. Only if the inhabitants of the New World lost their connection with the light, would they, like Atlantis of old, be destroyed.

This vision of new possibilities inspired the Europeans as they considered the potential of North America. At a time when Europe was in the throes of the Hundred Years' War and the Thirty Years' War; when the continent was burdened by conflicting monarchies and empires struggling for land, riches, and power; and when, simultaneously, the seeds of the Enlightenment were being sown by the French scientist Renée Descartes, a contemporary of Bacon's, North America was seen as the locus of immense human possibility. What Europe was not, America could become. *New Atlantis* inspired people to believe that practical perfection was possible, and it was in this spirit that they flocked to American shores.

Many of those leaving Europe to explore the virgin lands and untapped potential of the New World actually called it the "New Atlantis." Others referred to it as the "New Athens," the "New Rome," the "New Israel," and the "New Jerusalem." America became the "promised land" where the best of Western civilization was distilled into a grand exploration of human possibility. It was an experiment based on a radical notion of freedom: that every single person has the God-given right to life, liberty, and the pursuit of happiness, and that final sovereignty rests not with the government but with the individual.

As Thomas Paine proclaimed, America was the place *to begin the world over again.* It was upon this rock that the United States was built. The possibility of pure freedom, based on individual sovereignty, was the elixir that ignited a social revolution first in America, then in France, and in our time, around the world.

The founding fathers of the United States were acutely aware of their historic political as well as spiritual responsibility. George

Washington, Thomas Jefferson, Benjamin Franklin, James Madison, among numerous others, were all revolutionaries. They were also members of the Masonic order, a secret society dedicated to the teachings of mystical Christianity. They were steeped in the political thinking of Locke, Smith, and Hume; they were schooled in the Enlightenment thinking of Descartes, Voltaire, and Montesquieu; they were immersed in the esoteric teachings of ancient Egypt, Greece, and Rome; and they were devoted to the scientific method and mystical writings of Bacon.

As they fought the Revolutionary War and as they created the Constitution of the United States, the founding fathers brought these strands together to achieve a whole new kind of nation, based on a radically new notion of human possibility. As Washington put it, America was to become what freemasonry already was—*a temple of virtue.* The United States was the first nation in history to be consciously created as a place of perfection.

The Great Seal of the United States, printed on every dollar bill, summarizes the great promise that the United States was founded to embody. It depicts a pyramid that the ancient Egyptians used as a metaphor for the tip of a beam of light. At the top of the pyramid is the all-seeing eye of Horus, the Egyptian sun god, whose essence is light and who represents the eye of knowledge. Underneath the pyramid are inscribed the words *Novus ordo seclorum,* which means "New order for the ages."

In this spirit, the founding fathers intended the United States to be the greatest of nations, destined to be an inspiration to all other nations and a beacon of freedom to the rest of the world. Benjamin Franklin summarized this vision when he said that America's true destiny was not to be about power, it was to be about light.

AMERICA'S MARCH TO POWER   The United States soon discovered that having such a foundation in the light gave it an extraordinary wisdom in the acquisition of power. Right from the beginning, even before the Revolutionary War in 1776, the Americans demonstrated remarkable agility in their interactions with the British, then the dominant European power. Alone among all the

British colonies, the Americans successfully broke away, something that the other British colonies would not accomplish for
nearly another two centuries.

In the immediate aftermath of the Revolutionary War, however, the founding fathers realized that the Continental Congress
they had set up under the Articles of Confederation was unable to
conduct effective foreign policy. The ability of the central government to do so was the primary reason put forth by James Madison,
Benjamin Franklin, and several others for ratifying the U.S. Constitution in 1789. In 1787, Thomas Jefferson wrote: "My idea is
that we should be made one nation in every case concerning foreign affairs, and separate ones in what is merely domestic."[14] This
principle, codified in the Constitution, birthed the American
republic and set it on its way to empire.

Even though the newly formed nation was vastly weaker than
its European counterparts, it nevertheless capitalized on its vic-
tory against the British and immediately exploited the tensions in
European politics to build a coalition against the British, appealing
to all nations to follow the norms of international law. This was followed by shrewd positioning and adaptability during the
Napolenonic Wars, so that when those wars had ended the United
States emerged with the greatest of the spoils—the Louisiana
Purchase. The U.S. acquisition of this territory deprived the
French of their New World empire and greatly added to the size of
the United States, pushing westward.

Over the next several decades, American diplomacy succeeded
in outmaneuvering the European powers on numerous occasions.
The Monroe Doctrine proclaimed that the entire Western Hemisphere was off-limits to foreign powers. The United States
annexed Florida and extended its boundary all the way across
North America to the Pacific. It opened Japan to world trade,
thwarted British efforts to turn Texas into a colony, and acquired
the Southwest by defeating Mexico in war.

During the Civil War, American diplomacy once again triumphed over European stratagems to divide and conquer the new
republic, successfully thwarting repeated efforts by the British
and the French to intervene on the side of the Confederacy. This

entailed not taking action when the British seized Confederate commissioners in the *Trent* affair but firmly compelling Britain to observe the principles of neutrality and pay compensation over Confederate ships built by British firms. As a result, the Union was preserved and the Europeans kept at bay.

Within a generation of the Civil War, the United States had consolidated unchallenged hegemony over the entire Western Hemisphere and had thereby established itself as a world power, though still much weaker than the British, then at the height of its imperial strength. The United States emerged from the scourge of World War I, however, with fewer casualties than any other great power and with fewer forces on the ground in Europe than the continental armies but with a greater voice in the peace that was to follow. More fundamentally, monarchical government in Europe disappeared after the Great War. As Mead puts it, "The great thrones and royal houses that once mocked the United States and its democratic pretensions vanished from the earth."[15]

Mead goes on to point out that despite the failure of the Treaty of Versailles, the principles enunciated by President Wilson survived the subsequent anarchy and chaos caused by the rise of fascism and bolshevism and continue to guide European and global politics even in the present day. These are the principle of democratic governance and the principle that collective security and the viability of international law can be ensured most effectively by the nations of the world coming together to form an international body. Wilson was the direct antecedent to Roosevelt, not only molding the world in 1918 as Roosevelt did in 1945 but also creating the foundation upon which Roosevelt later built.

The United States also emerged from the First World War as the world's wealthiest nation. Germany—America's greatest economic rival—had been devastated by both the war and the Treaty of Versailles. Neither Britain nor France could any longer mount effective opposition to American designs. In fact, in the aftermath of the war, Britain conceded to the United States something it had withheld from any of its European rivals for more than two centuries: it accepted the United States as an equal power of the seas with the right to mount a navy as large as Britain's. Where both

Napoleon and Wilhelm II had failed, Wilson and Harding succeeded, and they did so without firing a single shot against the British. A diplomatic effort that asserted American interests while emphasizing the common values between the two nations had persuaded Great Britain to accept peacefully the equality that no rival previously had been able to compel by force.

The results of the Second World War were essentially the same. The United States entered later than any other major power, suffered the fewest casualties, and realized the greatest gains. Churchill fought heroically against Hitler, Mussolini, and Hirohito but was trumped by Roosevelt. Stalin was certainly able to expand westward and seize the devastated eastern portion of Europe, but the Americans more quickly achieved unchallenged, even welcome hegemony over western Europe, the bloc of nations that constituted the wealthiest, most dynamic, and intellectually advanced region on earth.

Forty years later, after an intense rivalry, the Soviet bloc disintegrated and the Soviet Union broke up. In the meantime, the U.S. dollar had become the international medium of commerce, English had become the common parlance of world business and science, and American consumer products and culture dominated world markets. When the Berlin Wall fell in 1989, the United States stood alone at the pinnacle of power and influence, its values informing the global consensus and its will shaping international affairs.

This march to the pinnacle of power may seem at first glance to have been an easy and straightforward trajectory, something Americans gained without really paying the price. But empires are never gained without great determination, sacrifice, and bloodshed, particularly empires such as Rome and America, which march to the front rank of empires and gain the status of power without peer. Virtually every president in American history has sent troops abroad or faced some kind of crisis with European or Asian powers, and American society has felt and been shaped by the effects of these engagements, even if living in the "splendid isolation" that the protection of two vast oceans and weak neighbors afforded.

During the Napoleonic Wars, for example, America fought a declared naval war against France and both declared and undeclared wars against Great Britain. These wars had enormous effects on American society. Some historians consider the total embargo President Jefferson placed on trade between the United States and Europe to be one of the most painful economic traumas Americans have ever experienced. The War of 1812 almost broke the newly formed republic apart as the British sacked Washington, attacked Baltimore and New Orleans, and blockaded the entire eastern seaboard of the United States. In the face of this, American foreign investment fell 90 percent between 1807 and 1814. The resulting collapse of the prices for American agricultural products, especially cotton and tobacco, forced untold numbers of Americans into bankruptcy and ruin.

Between the War of 1812 and the Civil War, the United States was acutely aware of its relative weakness compared with European powers and lived in a virtual permanent war atmosphere, during which time the European powers were either threatening war or levying sanctions against it. U.S. forces were deployed not only in North and South America but in Africa and Asia as well.

During the entire nineteenth century, the United States struggled militarily and diplomatically with Europe, particularly with Great Britain, always from the vantage point of the weaker against the stronger. A substantial part of the American defense budget went to build an impressive string of forts up and down the eastern coast. Many were used during the Civil War, some remain operational to the present day.

During the administration of President Martin van Buren (1837 to 1840), the United States supported Irish and Canadian rebels against the British in Canada, and this almost brought the two old rivals to war yet again. Then a dispute arose between Maine and New Brunswick in 1840, which led to the "Aroostock War," in which both Britain and the United States deployed troops in the area. At the same time, the British were maneuvering to bring the newly independent state of Texas inside the British sphere of influence, which triggered the U.S. annexation of Texas and served as instigation for the war against Mexico. Just as this war was subsiding, a conflict broke out in the Northwest in 1848 along what is now the Oregon border. Again the conflict was with the British over competing territorial claims, leading to the "Fifty Four Forty or Fight" slogan, which dominated the elections of 1848.

The 1850s saw another spate of conflicts with the British, as southerners sought to establish new slave states in Cuba and Nicaragua while the British were extending their control along both the Atlantic and Pacific coasts of Central America in order to better coordinate communication among their far-flung colonial holdings. By this time, the British had taken up the antislavery campaign, and so their efforts to search American ships for slaves and their refusal to return any slaves they found contributed to constant antagonisms. But as soon as the Civil War broke out, the British sided with the Confederacy, allowing the southern navy to outfit its boats in British harbors and seeking in numerous ways to ensure the breakup of the Union.

Napoleon III of France joined the British in siding with the South and maneuvering to destroy the Union. His establishment of a puppet emperor in Mexico was the boldest move any European power ever made to contest the Monroe Doctrine. However, immediately after General Lee's surrender at Appomatox in 1865, General Ulysses Grant dispatched victorious Union troops to the Rio Grande. France withdrew its forces, leaving the defenseless "Emperor" Maximilian to be shot by a Mexican firing squad in 1867.

At the same time the United States was forcing the French out of Mexico, it was dealing with Russians coming down from the north. Secretary of State William Seward made the historic purchase of Alaska from the Russian czar in 1867. It was ridiculed as "Seward's folly" at the time, but turned out to be one of the vitally important acquisitions in American history. It gave the United States a huge piece of land strategically placed against the British in the Northwest, and it pushed the Russians entirely out of the Western Hemisphere and back into Siberia.

The United States also contested European, mostly Spanish power in Latin America, sending troops as early as 1832 to the

Falkland Islands to reduce an Argentine garrison that was harass-
ing American ships. Between the Civil War and the Spanish-
American War of 1898, the United States sent Marines to
Argentina, Chile, Colombia, Cuba, Haiti, and Uruguay.

In its march to supremacy, the fledgling American republic
was even bold enough to deploy troops beyond the Western
Hemisphere across the two vast oceans that separated it from the
rest of the world. In 1813, President Jefferson sent troops to the
South Pacific to the Marquesas Islands, and in 1815, to Tripoli and
Algiers to deal with the Barbary pirates. President Jackson sent
troops to Sumatra to shell and burn the coastal town of Quallah
Bttoo. In 1843 and 1860, U.S. troops were sent to Liberia to protect American interests.

In 1843, American troops landed in Canton to protect Americans from hostile Chinese, returning in 1860 to defeat five thousand Chinese troops in pitched battle and establish a permanent
American military presence there. In 1871, U.S. Marines attacked
Korea, seizing two forts in a punitive expedition. Even while the
Civil War raged, President Lincoln dispatched troops to Japan and
Panama. By 1900, the United States had established a military
presence in the South Pacific sufficient to weather an international crisis with Germany over control of Sumatra.

In and through all these military expeditions, the American
republic swept "from sea to shining sea," uniting the forty-eight
states into a single nation, consolidating hegemony over North,
Central, and South America, and establishing the beginnings of a
global military presence. A permanent naval squadron in the
Mediterranean Sea was established in 1815, initially to keep the
Barbary pirates at bay, but then maintained in perpetuity. This was
followed in 1822 with the establishment of permanent naval
squadrons in the Caribbean and Pacific, charged with protecting
American whalers and commercial interests in Latin America and
the South Pacific. In 1826, naval squadrons were established to
protect American interests in the South Atlantic, and in 1835, a
squadron was established off the west coast of Africa.

The point of all this history is to underscore the deep imperial
impulse of American history. From its very inception, and even

during the Civil War, the United States deployed forces on every major continent of the world, sent its navy to sail every ocean, and maintained dynamic diplomatic relations with the prevailing empires of the eighteenth and nineteenth centuries. It may seem that the events of the twentieth century with its two world wars and military confrontation with the Soviet Union involved the United States in world affairs to an unprecedented degree, but the fact is that the late eighteenth and the entire nineteenth century saw Americans equally if not more involved internationally. This involvement from the very beginning was to build a global presence to protect American interests.

Mead points out that of the first nine presidents of the republic, six served initially as secretary of state and seven as ambassadors abroad. Four of the first twelve—George Washington, Andrew Jackson, William Harrison, and Zachary Taylor—were elected principally because of their leadership abilities in the field against foreign enemies. Six of the American presidents who served before the Civil War had been both secretary of state and ambassador to Great Britain, then the highest foreign diplomatic assignment. Thomas Jefferson had been secretary of state and ambassador to France, and John Adams had been ambassador to both Great Britain and France.

In contrast, few American presidents during the twentieth century had foreign experience prior to becoming president. Only two had any lengthy foreign experience: Dwight Eisenhower, who served as supreme commander of the Allied forces in World War II, and George Bush, Sr., who was director of the Central Intelligence Agency and ambassador to China.

The reason for America's early and continuous involvement in foreign affairs was a simple one: the prosperity of American society was inextricably tied to international commerce and trade. This was true from even before the inception of the republic. As colonies, American products were sent to Europe, mostly to Great Britain. This did not change after the Revolutionary War. The U.S. economy was as dependent on foreign trade in 1790 as it was in 1990; indeed, during the nineteenth century it was even more dependent than it was during the twentieth. As a percentage of the gross domestic product, foreign trade accounted for 13.4 percent from 1869 to 1893, whereas during the years 1945 to 1989, it accounted for only 7.3 percent.

Furthermore, foreign trade did not simply dominate the cities and towns of the eastern seaboard. During the eighteenth and nineteenth centuries, more than half of all Americans were engaged in agriculture, and agricultural products flowed from America's heartland across the Atlantic to European consumers. Even in remote settlements on the western frontier, international trade was integral to prosperity. Between 1802 and 1860, cotton exports rose in value from $5 million a year to $192 million; by 1900, the value had reached $213 million. A full two-thirds of these exports went to British manufacturers. As pioneers settled the Midwest, wheat exports became important also, averaging $88 million annually between 1865 and 1900. Between 1850 and 1900, agricultural goods made up roughly three-quarters of all U.S. exports.

Foreign markets also had a significant impact on the new republic. The economic depression that followed the Napoleonic Wars in Europe spread to the United States. The U.S. financial panic of 1837 had its origins in England and caused several states, particularly Pennsylvania, to default on their bonds. Similarly, the financial panic of 1857 began in the aftermath of the Crimean War, when troubles on the French exchange spread to London and from there to New York.

This interconnectivity was further heightened in 1866 with the completion of the transatlantic cable, which allowed essentially instantaneous communication by telegraph across the Atlantic. Even more than before, the U.S. economy became vulnerable to the shocks and collapses of various European financial markets. During 1893, for instance, the collapse of the Argentine loan market adversely affected British banks, which in turn caused panic on Wall Street.

So tied was the U.S. economy to the world that even as American diplomats were fighting with certain Europeans, they were borrowing from others. President Jefferson made the Louisiana Purchase by paying the French with money he borrowed from the

Dutch. Half the national debt during his presidency was owed to foreign interests. Over 30 percent of the money used to build the great canals in the early 1800s came from Europe. This was also true for the building of the American railroads and the establishment of cattle ranching. By 1800, foreign interests owned over twenty million acres of ranch land along the western frontier.

When we think of Davy Crockett or Daniel Boone roaming the wilds of Appalachia, or of the pioneers rumbling inexorably westward fighting the Indians and settling the land, we do not usually remember that foreign money was often involved. Overseas markets were usually the destination point for any goods sent back East, making the general economic condition of the American economy dependent on the vicissitudes of European markets.

American economic interests also affected other nations, especially as the nineteenth century wore on. Virtually all the incursions by American troops into Latin America during the nineteenth and twentieth centuries were to protect or extend American business interests. The various naval squadrons were deployed to secure American commercial trade routes. So skillfully and ruthlessly was this done that by the end of the First World War, America had emerged as the dominant economic power in the world. This was followed by the Great Depression of the 1930s, when the collapse of the American stock market affected the entire world economy. From the Second World War on, the American economy has driven the global economy and American corporations have dominated the global marketplace.

The oceans that protected America *from* the world have also served as its highways *to* the world. Americans have traversed these oceans from the very beginning with both commerce and troops, reinforced by a deep and abiding belief in America's manifest destiny. Americans have carried out this mission so skillfully and with such perseverance that, two hundred years after its birth, America has emerged as the wealthiest and most powerful nation on earth.

4

The Roots of American Preeminence

TAKING INTO ACCOUNT AMERICA'S COMMITMENT to light and ascent to power, the question must be asked: Why did the United States rise to empire and to world supremacy? Why did the United States, rather than Brazil or China or Russia, achieve this preeminence? What strands of the American past, when taken together, explain its extraordinary success as a nation and as an empire?

This is virtually an impossible question to answer in the present. Historians in the future will have to look back on the American empire as we do upon Britain, Athens, or Rome before any clarity will emerge. Even then, they will argue about America as they still do about the whys and wherefores of the rise and fall of other empires. People are constrained by history because they are contained within history. This constraint deepens the pathos of the experience but inhibits the capacity for perspective.

Nevertheless, there are three essential reasons for the American success, which explain something of its uniqueness among the nations and its inordinate aggregation of imperial power: its British heritage, its Athenian heritage, and its relentless application of military force.

AMERICA'S BRITISH HERITAGE   The first and most fundamental point about the rise of the United States as a world power is that it was graced by God and history to be a colony of Great Britain rather than any of the powers of continental Europe. The British Empire was the most elegantly maintained, benignly governed, and commercially oriented of all the European empires. This could only be so of a tiny island nation the fraction of the size of the mighty empire it built. For the United States as a colony, Britain was not so much an oppressive overlord as an exemplary teacher. Britain taught America the ways of empire, eventually to become its closest ally and friend.

If we look back on the rise of the American empire, it has always been closely intertwined with Great Britain. Mead makes this point, dividing the history of American foreign policy into four eras, all based on America's changing relationship with Great Britain. The first era lasted from 1776 to 1823, during which the Americans, having won their independence *from* Britain were preoccupied with working out their relationship *with* Britain, then approaching its own apogee moment of world dominion. The British had to decide whether the newly established republic was to be undermined as an enemy or developed as an ally and trading partner. The Americans had to decide whether to form alliances to undermine their former master or to side with Britain in its imperial struggles against the French and the Spanish.

What emerged was a tense relationship of competition and confrontation that led to the War of 1812. However, beneath the conflict was the determination by the British that it was better to have a stable trading partnership with the Americans than to add them to their list of enemies, already long and comprising continental Europeans, especially Napoleon. The Americans, while resisting British advances in North America, came to believe that it was better to have the British rule the waves than any of the other Europeans, who were more severe and cruel in their imperial policies.

What brought this era to a close was the promulgation of the Monroe Doctrine in 1823, which declared that the Western Hemisphere was essentially off-limits to further encroachments by

European colonialism. The motivation was, in part, to help the British prevent the French or the Spanish from reestablishing dynastic empires in the Western Hemisphere after the revolutionary movements in Latin America had gained independence for most of that continent. In part, too, America wanted to signal to Europe generally that the United States had by then emerged as a serious power with its own imperial ambitions and that the future of the New World was to be under American protection and exploitation.

The second era lasted from 1823 to 1914. During this time the United States was content to exist in a British-dominated international system and pursue policies worldwide that opened markets for American goods and services. Britain was clearly the senior partner, although the Treaty of Washington in 1871 demarcated the moment at which the United States succeeded in negotiating a treaty to its advantage. It was awarded $15.5 million in damages to Union shipping during the Civil War by confederate ships built by the British. It was during this time that U.S. policy planners and strategists first began to think about a world beyond *pax Britannica* and to formulate American designs for a more active world policy. The acquisition of bases and fueling stations throughout the Pacific was part of the American preparations for a post-British world order.

The third era, from 1914 to 1945, encompassed the two world wars of the twentieth century. As a result of World War I, Britain lost 22 percent of its national territory (Ireland), incurred debts equivalent to 136 percent of its gross domestic product, and suffered unemployment and inflation rates not experienced in over a century. The United States was thus forced to wrestle with all the issues of an ascendant empire. With the British visibly in decline, should the United States prop them up? Should the United States just withdraw and let the world situation sort itself out without undue American influence? Or should the United States prepare to replace the British as the world superpower?

The decisions made on these questions have shaped the world ever since. It was clear by 1945 that the British were finished as an imperial power. It was Franklin Roosevelt's genius to grasp this moment and project American supremacy to the world. As Mead puts it, "No reptilian brain could have dealt as unsentimentally with an old friend as Roosevelt and the U.S. Treasury Department dealt with Churchill's government." He also observes, however, that "the Americans dismantled the British Empire without fighting a war against it, and in fact while defending it against other, much more brutal enemies."[1]

Viewed from this perspective, Mead is correct in saying that "the fall of the British Empire was the most important event in international politics in the twentieth century, and in the whole history of American foreign policy."[2] The two world wars, even the Cold War, were really wars for the British succession, as Germany, Japan, the Soviet Union, and the United States competed to inherit the British mantle of global hegemony. In effect, the two world wars were fundamentally framed by the struggle between the United States and Germany for supremacy. The United States won this competition. It assisted in the dismantling of the dying British Empire, fought off the other competitors, and established the basis of the new international order in which the United States replaced the British as the central player.

The Cold War with the Soviet Union, as critical as it was, was only a theater in this larger competition. It was not an event in and of itself. It was almost a side show, for the United States emerged from the Cold War as it had entered it, with undisputed world power.

The Americans learned from the British the importance of commerce over territory and the inherent dangers of colonialism and direct political control. The British bequeathed to the Americans the centrality of freedom of the seas, the sanctity of property and commerce, the critical role of local oligarchs, and the importance of using military might to enforce commercial agreements. These were principles on which British rule was based. Enforcing them with a navy that dominated the oceans, the British held sway. It was America's refinement of these principles and practices that contributed to its attainment of supremacy when the British Empire declined and fell.

For the seafaring British, imperial power invariably began as a commercial venture. North America was first explored and exploited by the Hudson Bay Company. During the sixteenth century, when freebooters and pirates had seized much of the Caribbean from the Spanish, the British navy was sent in to secure British commercial interests. They did so by enforcing the first modern international law, then primarily agreements among European powers.

The first seventy-five years of British presence in India were mediated through the East India Company, which operated as an independent commercial operation until the Crown partially took it over in 1773 because of financial problems. Only after the Indian Mutiny of 1856 did the Crown completely take over the company and therefore the rule of India. The prime minister at the time, Lord Palmerston, said that British imperial ambitions were characterized by "trade without rule where possible; trade with rule where necessary."[3]

After the building of the Suez Canal in 1870, considered the jewel in the British Imperial Crown, Britain established a strong naval presence in the eastern Mediterranean and Persian Gulf but without directly taking over much territory. A typical instance occurred in Egypt in 1876 after it defaulted on loans owed to European, mostly British, banks. An Anglo-French fleet sailed up the Nile and installed direct control over Egyptian national finances, but left the government and monarchy in place.

British rule throughout the Persian Gulf was similarly indirect. The Bank of Persia, for example, was founded and run by English investors while Persia itself remained independent. When the emirs of Aden refused to build a lighthouse required by the British navy along the Red Sea, the P&O Steamship Company built and managed it, but the British did not colonize Aden. Only in Africa did the British establish direct colonial rule from the beginning.

It was their skillful use of sea power that enabled the British to rule so many lands so indirectly, and even then their actual troop strength was small. Until the South Africa War of 1899 to 1902, and then the First World War, which necessitated more ground strength, there were never more than 150,000 troops in the entire British army. This is a much smaller number than the Pentagon routinely stations overseas today. At the height of imperial power in 1897, the security of the empire was provided by 40,000 British troops, supported by an additional 310,000 local recruits, mostly in India, coming to some 350,000, roughly the size of the Roman army at its peak under the emperor Trajan in the second century.

Mostly through the projection of their naval power, the British were able to maintain the most diverse and far-flung empire in history and to ensure freedom of the seas for international commerce. Under the benign rule of Britannia, the oceans of the world became a common good for all seafarers. The guns of the Royal Navy ensured that sovereign states that borrowed money, usually from British banks in London, and then did not repay the debt, were forced to do so. The British navy would sail up, troops would land, seize the port and the customs operations, and impose direct tariffs and duties, as happened in Egypt, until the debt was repaid.

Similarly, when the property of British citizens was threatened or destroyed by local riots and rebellions, British troops were often dispatched until order was restored and British interests were secured. Again, Lord Palmerston: "As the Roman, in days of old, held himself free from indignity, when he could say 'Civis Romanus sum,' so also a British subject, in whatever land he may be, shall feel confident that the watchful eye and the strong arm of England will protect him against injustice and wrong."[4]

With freedom of the seas assured by military might, the British traded and prospered. British investors financed the railroads of the American West, the cattle farms of Argentina, and the gold mines of South Africa. Ships were launched from the rivers Clyde and Tyne, powered by Welsh coal and insured by Lloyd's of London. The Reuters news service informed customers around the world of the commodity prices in the universal currency of the British gold standard as produced by London's Royal Mint. Everything was available for exchange, from the ships to the coal to the gold coins, to anyone who was willing to transact the deal in English, abide by British enforced international law, and participate in an economic system in which the British were the exporting and importing customer of first and last resort.

It is worth noting that for all the benefits they provided during their apogee moment, the British were as intensely disliked then as the Americans are today. Robert Laird Collier, an American traveler, made this observation about the British during a trip to England in the 1880s: "No people are so disliked out of their own country. They assume superiority. As a nation they are intensely selfish and arrogant."[5]

An essential reason for the success of American foreign policy is that, following Britain, the United States has been motivated fundamentally by resources and trade, not territory. Indeed, we could say that it is a predominantly commercial motivation that has made Americans so pragmatic and relentless. This has proved to be both a crucial distinction, particularly from the continental European powers, and a critical advantage, especially in the age of globalization. Most empires have been motivated fundamentally by territorial gain and military supremacy in the context of a zero-sum game. This preoccupied the French, Russian, Austro-Hungarian, Portuguese, and Spanish empires far more than it did the British. If the Portuguese lost territory to the Spanish in South America, then Portugal felt weakened, and vice versa. This general policy of military and territorial competition kept these empires in constant conflict and subordinated the free flow of trade and capital between them.

This distinction is important because commercial interests tend to operate completely differently than territorial and military interests. Commercial interests succeed over the long term only to the degree that buyer and seller are both satisfied, no matter their political differences. Furthermore, increases in productivity and wealth generally emerge when many parties participate in the transactions and enjoy the benefits. This implies that contacts and trade with friends and enemies alike are to be valued, and it tends to generate policies that tolerate differences for the sake of capital flow and the generation of wealth.

Separated by two vast oceans, and therefore out of the theater of territorial competition with Europe, the United States emphasized from its inception the importance of commerce. It has been loss of trade rather than loss of territory that has most preoccupied the United States during its rise to empire. The demands for freedom of the seas, the promulgation of open-door policies, and more recently, the negotiations for free trade zones always have been at the core of America's expansion around the world.

Indeed, it has been characteristic of American imperialism that it took territories only reluctantly, preferring to use its military might to open markets and ensure commercial advantage rather than administer foreign states. While the European powers, including the British, got bogged down in holding lands far distant from their shores at an enormous cost in money, time, and lives, the Americans quite skillfully avoided territorial control for commercial advantage. Money, not land, has always been at the core of American imperial designs. When the modern era of globalization began, this put the Americans at enormous strategic advantage. Money moves; land does not.

THE LIGHT OF ATHENIAN DEMOCRACY   The second major reason for America's extraordinary rise to power also has roots in Britain, but more deeply, in the legacy of Athens. It is Athens that inspired Bacon and the founding fathers, and it is to Athens that America owes the democratic design of its government and the democratic nature of its foreign policy formation. The founding fathers of the United States claim the title for the greatest genius applied to the *design* of good government. In this, they were students of Athens.

The Declaration of Independence, which launched the Revolutionary War against Great Britain in 1776, declared the "unalienable" right of individuals to "life, liberty and the pursuit of happiness." These principles of human equality and freedom were codified in the U.S. Constitution, ratified by the newly liberated colonies in 1789, and have been embedded in America's political and social genetic coding ever since.

More than any nation in the modern era, the United States has upheld democratic ideals in its internal development as well as in its foreign policy. Integral to its imperial strategy has been the mission of spreading democracy and human rights around the world. This has had a deep shadow side, as the next chapter will explore, but for all its failures, American democracy has shined with a greater light than any other since the time of Athens.

In this sense, America is as much the successor to Athens as it is to Great Britain. Athens was the original model of a free trading empire extended and protected by a strong navy. It was also the first city-state and empire to embrace democracy as its form of government, along with a vaunted sense of mission to bring the light of civilization to a dark barbarian world. Athens bequeathed to the world the importance of vision.

Even to this day, historians consider Periclean Athens to be the apogee moment of human civilization, a humbling thought for those who consider modernity—or postmodernity as we like to think of our time—to be the highest point in the human journey. We are certainly the *furthest* point in that journey but the *highest* point actually happened twenty-five hundred years ago in the environs of the Acropolis. As the poet Shelley put it, "The period which intervened between the birth of Pericles and the death of Aristotle is undoubtedly, whether considered in itself or with reference to the effect which it has produced upon the subsequent destinies of civilized man, the most memorable in the history of the world."[6]

Two credos framed and characterized Athenian greatness. The first was articulated by the philosopher Protagoras: "Man is the measure of all things." The second came from the philosopher Anaxagoras: "All things were in confusion until Mind came and set them in order."[7] Of all the peoples of antiquity, it was the Athenians during the fifth century B.C. who originated the notions that humanity, not the gods, was the center of all things, and that mind was the center of what it meant to be human. The supreme command of the Greeks was that of the Delphic oracle, made immortal by Socrates: "Know thyself." Out of this profound insight came the first democratic impulse in history and the flowering of a culture centered around the pursuit of truth, beauty, and goodness that influences us to the present day.

The Athenians' courage to place humanity at the center of the universe was inextricably tied to their history and their heroic resistance to the imperial expansion of Persia, then the world's superpower. The Persian emperor Darius and his son Xerxes sought to extend their empire beyond Anatolia into Greece. But in

490 B.C., when the huge Persian army, outnumbering the Greeks by five to one, descended upon Attica, they were defeated by a miniscule force of Athenians in the battle of Marathon. This feat was repeated in the year 480 B.C., when a tiny band of three hundred Spartans held back twenty-thousand Persians at the pass of Thermopylae. Finally came the battle of Salamis, in which the Athenians, vastly outnumbered by the largest army assembled until the twentieth century, defeated the Persians yet again.

These victories freed Europe from the threat of Asiatic domination for fifteen hundred years and released the first impulse of humanism that came to full flower between 480 and 399 B.C. This was the golden age of Athens. Under the guidance of Pericles, whom the historian Will Durant calls the "commander in chief of all the physical and spiritual forces of Athens during her greatest age,"[8] Athens embarked on history's first exploration of democratic governance, elevated by the heights of her philosophy and inspired by the realism of her art. Athens imprinted Western civilization at its inception with a model that was rebellious in its instinct and democratic in its practice.

Such was the power of the light emanating from the Acropolis that long after Alexander's empire had turned to dust and Athens had been conquered by the Romans, the beacon of democracy radiated outward through antiquity to influence Rome in building its republic. Undimmed, it moved forward into history to inspire the British when King John signed the Magna Carta at Runnymede in 1215 and when the Americans drafted the U.S. Constitution in Philadelphia in 1787. At their deepest level of destiny, the British first and then the Americans are carriers of the Athenian light. Both are Athens *recidivus*.

History remembers Athens for its democracy, philosophy, drama, and mathematics, even as it recognizes Britain for Shakespeare, Parliamentary democracy, a free press, and jury trials. America has taken these traditions forward and led the movement, now some two and a half millennia old, to democratize the world. Whereas only a few nations were democratic when the American republic was established, now only a few are explicitly nondemocratic as America reaches its point of empire.

This is not to say that all is well. As Churchill reminded his contemporaries, democracy is the worst form of government, except for all the others. But it is to say that what began as a philosophical experiment in Athens twenty-five hundred years ago has now, through the inspiration of Britain and the power of the United States, become the single most dominant human commitment as applied to governance.

This commitment to freedom and democracy gave America its sense of mission in the world, a crucial component in its reach for empire. If Greece and Rome sought to tame the "barbarians" and Britain and France sought to bring civilization to the "natives," the United States has sought to bring freedom to an unfree world.

Envisioning a nation of light did not mean being naive about society or governance. Following the teachings of Bacon and the political philosopher Thomas Hobbes, the founding fathers were profoundly realistic about human nature, understanding that government had to take it into account, not try to change it. As Madison put it in *The Federalist Papers*, "The *causes* of faction cannot be removed and . . . relief is only to be sought in the means of controlling its *effects*."[9] He believed that human nature would always be competitive and fractious, and that the only thing government could do was seek to modify human behavior. Alexander Hamilton agreed, arguing that the natural anarchistic and combative tendencies of human beings will always remain and can only be countered by a strong central government.

The genius of the founding fathers is that they realized that the corruption of human nature would, if left unchecked, corrupt the power of government itself. They therefore went to great lengths to ensure that the government they created was kept untyrannical in its governance of a people who naturally would resist control.

"In framing a government," Madison wrote, "the great difficulty lies in this: you must first enable the government to control the governed; and in the next place oblige it to control itself. A dependence on the people is, no doubt, the primary control on the government; but experience has taught mankind the necessity of auxiliary precautions."[10] These precautions, which Madison called "inventions of prudence," became the checks and balances created by the framers of the Constitution to divide the government into three branches, one to legislate, one to execute, and one to judge, ensuring that none of them exercise inordinate power over the others.

They even took care to put in place temporal asymmetries in the Constitution to ensure that no crisis or public mood could unduly influence the entire system. The members of the House of Representatives are elected to two-year terms every two years. Senators are elected to six-year terms with staggered elections of one-third of the Senate every two years. The president is elected to four-year terms, and the Supreme Court justices serve for life.

The intent of this, said Madison, was to create a system "broken into so many parts, interests and classes of citizens, that the rights of the individuals, or of the minority, will be in little danger from interested combinations of the majority."[11] In giving this kind of fundamental sovereignty to the individual, in constructing a government with power but unable to rule despotically, in creating a vision of human dignity and equality embedded in the divine order itself, the founding fathers birthed a republic the likes of which the world had never seen.

The United States has carried the light of freedom for the past two centuries. It is the first country in history to be populated almost entirely by people coming from somewhere else, almost all fleeing persecution, tyranny, and deprivation to create a new life with a new purpose in a new land. In this sense, the world came to America and America became the world. It has always represented more of a possibility to be lived than a country to which one belongs, an ideal to be attained rather than a fact to be endured. As Thomas Jefferson said, America was to be an "empire of liberty."[12]

Furthermore, from its inception, the United States has been viewed by Americans themselves as providentially blessed, imbued with a significance more sacred than mundane and having to do in its essence with a contract with freedom. As George Washington said in his first inaugural address: "The preservation of the sacred fire of liberty has been entrusted to the hands of the American people." Washington was clear to counsel the new republic not to promulgate the new fire as much as simply to protect it from being extinguished, but Americans marched westward across the continent and sailed around the world with the call to liberty on their lips. They felt called on a mission, as theologian Rheinhold Niebuhr put it, of "tutoring mankind on its pilgrimage to perfection."[13]

While from the beginning Americans viewed their development of democracy as a providential mission, Americans have carried forward this mission out of an equally profound sense of self-interest. Despite the rhetoric of freedom and democracy, Americans have never seen the establishment of their power as an altruistic enterprise. Rather, American policymakers and the public alike have viewed the promotion of freedom around the world as the most effective way of ensuring that American interests would remain secure.

As American interests became more global in scope, American democratic ideals, always viewed as universal, and American interests, generally commercial, became inextricably interlinked and functionally synonymous. American light and American power became increasingly intertwined. The successive campaigns to advance American ideals—whether against the Germans in World War I, the Germans again and the Japanese in World War II, or the Soviets during the Cold War—all resulted in extending the boundaries of freedom and in aggregating more American military, economic, and political power. When it was all over, free market capitalism and democracy were global and America stood as a colossus astride the globe.

America's emphasis on commerce gave it a critical advantage in an age of economic globalization. Its commitment to democratic ideals enabled it to lead the historical process of democratization. At the time of its inception in the late eighteenth century, free trade and democracy were definitely minority views, scarcely valued by the imperial powers of Europe caught up in the realpolitik of conquest and competition. It was America's great fortune and veritable genius that it staked its destiny and built its empire on the two most fundamental megatrends of the modern era— free trade and democratic governance—and intertwined its self-interest in the promulgation and establishment of both. For more than two hundred years, the United States has championed these causes and thus has had the good fortune of being supported by history, while the imperial powers of Europe, mired in monarchy, aristocracy, territorial ambitions, and military conflicts, were vanquished by the same history that brought the United States to the fore.

Not surprisingly, Americans now, like the British, Athenians, and Romans before them, view this distribution of power as basically a divine affirmation that the United States has been "on the right side of history," as President Clinton was fond of saying and the Bush administration assumes. American preeminence is considered to be both a measure and a guarantee of humanity's long march toward democracy, freedom, and world peace. Nations thinking otherwise are considered "rogue states"—enemies of America and of freedom itself. It is this view that inspires the new American internationalism of George W. Bush.

THE RELENTLESS APPLICATION OF AMERICAN MILITARY FORCE   There is a third reason for the American rise to global dominance, one the Bush administration has specifically sought to advance: the United States has supported its interests in commerce and its commitment to democracy with a bold and relentless application of military force. Compared with its competitors and with empires long past, the United States has developed the most effective and lethal military capacity in the history of the world.

This might come as a shock, mostly to Americans themselves, but the facts of American history demonstrate that the United States has relentlessly and brutally applied its military force to gain advantage as it spread across North America and around the world. Indeed, it has been its willingness to use military force with devastation and finality that has advanced its commercial interests, protected its democratic governance, secured its self-interests, and propelled it to the front rank of empires. As Paul Kennedy puts it, "From the time the first settlers arrived in Virginia from England and started moving westward, this was an imperial nation, a conquering nation."[14]

Internally, the United States Army engaged the native peoples of North America in battle more than 1,250 times as the pioneers relentlessly swept westward from the Atlantic seaboard to the Pacific. The U.S. military and the American settlers sought to eliminate the native peoples in much the same way as they sought to eliminate wild animals and pests from their farms and cities. All across the frontier, bounties were paid for Indians killed, a practice that lasted until well into the twentieth century in several western states. Surviving Native Americans were herded into the tribal reservations where many still live today.

It is worth noting, especially since President Bush ordered large-scale vaccinations against smallpox to protect Americans against bioterrorism in 2003, that the first recorded use of bioterrorism took place on June 24, 1763. The victims were Native Americans. The perpetrators were the British under General Amherst at Fort Pitt, in what is now upstate New York. Finding it difficult to defeat them militarily, the British called the Indians they were fighting to a parley, at the end of which they gave them two blankets and one handkerchief taken from a smallpox hospital. The Indian tribes were decimated by the plague, and the British consolidated control over the region. A century later, in the 1860s and 1870s, American settlers also traded to the Indians blankets deliberately infected with smallpox. Thousands of people, including entire tribes, were wiped out.

Externally, the United States has used military force on more than 235 occasions from the Revolutionary War in 1776 until the invasion of Iraq in 2003, if you count World War I, World War II, the Vietnam War, and so on, as single occasions. With the exception of the War of 1812 and Vietnam, the United States has never lost a war, a record that is without historical precedent in the modern era. In the course of American history, ten former generals have become president. Several additional presidents, such as George Bush, Sr., John Kennedy, and Theodore Roosevelt, while not becoming generals, were aided in their rise to the presidency by their war records.

Despite the image of a benign power, particularly to itself, the United States has used its military with overwhelming and often indiscriminate force. In the course of fighting foreign wars, the

United States has lost some 442,000 soldiers in combat. During the last five months of World War II alone, American bombing raids killed more than 900,000 Japanese civilians, not counting the atomic bombings of Hiroshima and Nagasaki, which added another 127,150 civilian deaths. During the night of March 9–10, 1945, 234 U.S. Air Force Superfortress bombers dropped some 1,167 tons of incendiary bombs over downtown Tokyo, killing an estimated 83,793 Japanese civilians. This one mission killed more people than the United States lost during the Korean and Vietnam wars combined, some 80,942. In the European theater of the war, the Anglo-American firebombing of Dresden, killing over 135,000, constituted the largest slaughter of civilians in one place at one time since the massacres of Genghis Khan in central Asia during the thirteenth century.

During the Korean War, the United States literally decimated North Korea, killing an estimated 1 million North Korean civilians out of a total population of 9.4 million. The Americans suffered 34,000 dead, giving them a kill ratio of over thirty to one.

During the Vietnam War, the United States dropped three times the explosive power that it did during all of World War II. Some 365,000 Vietnamese civilians are believed to have died against roughly 50,000 American deaths, giving a kill ratio of Vietnamese civilians to American soldiers of about seven to one. This ratio of civilian-to-combat deaths in these two wars exceeds that of the German onslaught against the Russians on the eastern front of the Second World War, which, in popular mythology, defines modern brutality. There the Germans inflicted some 10 million Russian civilian deaths and lost 2 million of their own soldiers, a civilian-soldier kill ratio of five to one.

The point here is that the United States has been a ruthless and often indiscriminate military power in the furtherance of its interests. It did not rise to world dominance by some immaculate conception, simply because it enjoyed trade and carried noble ideals to the far corners of the world. It rose to world dominance because in the first and last resort, it has applied its military force as effectively as its commercial interests and as relentlessly as its democratic ideals. The three taken together have built the U.S. global hegemony, and the three must remain together, in whatever combination, for the United States to keep itself in that position.

The American public has intuited this fact, and since the beginning of the republic, has generally supported waging war at the highest possible intensity until victory is ensured. From the massacres of the Native Americans, to General Sherman's fiery march to the sea in 1864–65, to the atomic bombings of Hiroshima and Nagasaki, the American public has broadly and continuously supported decisive military action, even if it is devastating and conducted against civilians. In this sense, Americans have been very much like the Romans, who were as relentless about victory as any empire ever built.

The American commitment to decisive military action has been matched by an equally strong commitment to large military budgets. In 1999, under the Clinton administration, the United States spent as much on its military as all its NATO allies, China, the Gulf states, Japan, Russia, and South Korea combined. Under the Bush administration, the United States spends virtually as much on the military as the fifteen to twenty leading nations combined, and there is a strong bipartisan support for ongoing huge military expenditures. The dramatic increase in military spending after 9/11 was done by acclamation.

Furthermore, Americans have consistently supported using the military forces these budgets make possible. For example, since the end of the Vietnam War, regarded by some as initiating an era of reluctance to use military force, the United States has deployed combat forces or used lethal force in Afghanistan, Albania, Bosnia, Cambodia, Grenada, Haiti, Iran, Iraq, Kuwait, Lebanon, Liberia, Libya, Macedonia, Panama, Saudi Arabia, Somalia, the South China Sea, Sudan, Turkey, and Yugoslavia.

Today, the U.S. military dominates the globe more decisively than any power in history. At the end of World War II, the United States had 1,139 bases around the world, 600 of which it closed immediately. Since then it has maintained roughly 600 on a permanent basis, about 400 in North America and Europe and some 200 in the rest of the world. It currently has roughly 650, with a major new complex developing in and around Iraq.

As mentioned earlier, what is unique about this military power is that it is used to protect commerce and further U.S. interests. It is rarely to control territory. No major empire in history has controlled less land than the Unites States does today. The United States has taken land reluctantly and given it up easily. In the 1990s, for example, when the government of the Philippines requested the return of Clark Air Force Base and the Subic Bay Naval Station, President Clinton turned over the bases to the Philippine military and the U.S. military quietly left. U.S. troops returned, welcomed by the Philippine government, in 2002 to fight alongside Philippine soldiers against guerilla groups linked to the al-Qaeda terrorist network. Similarly with the Panama Canal. Conceded by Colombia to the United States by the Hay-Herran Treaty of 1903, American money and engineers built and operated the canal until 1977 when President Carter returned it to the Panamanians and withdrew the American presence. But if American interests were ever threatened in the canal zone, U.S. troops would surely be back. Iraq will not be an exception. The United States will get its troops and personnel out as soon as it can while seeking to maintain economic and political influence, if not control.

Like Rome, unlike Athens, America was born to rule. Like Athens, unlike Rome, it was established to inspire. From Britain, the Americans learned to wear both these mantles lightly. From its inception, its destiny has been inextricably linked with that of the rest of the world. It has needed free markets to fuel its economy, it has championed the spread of democratic governance to guarantee its freedom, and it has used its military might to secure commercial access and victory over its enemies.

The insistence of U.S. presidents on free trade, democracy, and the right of the United States to use military power at the discretion of the United States is as fundamental to American history and the American psyche as motherhood and apple pie. The fact that George W. Bush, at the attainment of supreme power over the world, enunciated this doctrine yet again is consistent with what the United States has represented for more than two hundred years. It is why the United States became an empire. It constitutes the very essence of what being an American in the world has come to mean.

The potential tragedy of this is that while these principles might be consistent with American history, they are now inconsistent with the needs of an integrating world. As noted earlier, the world has changed fundamentally under the impact of instantaneous telecommunications and globalization. The relentless pursuit of free markets in the era of globalization has serious deleterious effects if left unregulated. The dogmatic application of democratic principles is not a simple and straightforward enterprise, especially in nations that are failing or so mired in debt and corruption that elections only perpetuate their problems. And the ruthless application of military might has less and less efficacy in a world in which cultural nuances and religious norms are more important than weapons in exerting influence and maintaining control.

The United States must reinvent all the traditions that brought it to greatness in order for it to retain its greatness. In order to do this, it must go back to the time before its pursuit of power to its experience with light, recalling the inspiring and cautionary tale of *New Atlantis*. Remember, Atlantis fell at its moment of global power. A reconnection with the light is absolutely key to America's future application of power, for in the face of a collapsing international order and a rising crescendo of interconnected global crises, a new global system must be envisioned and built. It is America's failure to grasp this necessity that constitutes the major part of its, and the world's, current danger.

5

Empire and Its Discontents

THE CHALLENGE TO AMERICAN LEADERSHIP today is that people around the world are increasingly experiencing America more as the enemy than as a friend, as Goliath rather than as David. Bewilderment about America, fear of America, even hatred of America are on the rise as people use American light to judge American power. In attaining so much power and in applying its power in such a highly militarized way, especially during the Cold War and since 9/11, it seems to many that the United States has betrayed its founding vision, as if in protecting the American dream at home, it has felt it necessary to deny its ideals abroad.

AMERICA'S DARK HISTORY IN IRAQ   The history of U.S. relations with Iraq provides an excellent case in point. Removing Saddam Hussein from power in 2003 was not the first time the United States engaged in regime change in Iraq. President Kennedy initiated the first one back in 1963.

In 1958, Iraqi leader Abdel Karim Kassem had overthrown a monarch friendly to the West, but he was tolerated by President Eisenhower because he provided a counterweight to Washington's nemesis of that era—Gamal Abdel Nasser of Egypt, who was stirring the Arab world with visions of national revival and power. But Kassem became a problem for Washington in 1961 when he began

93

to buy arms rivaling those of Israel, threatened Western oil interests, and talked openly of challenging American dominance in the
region. Kennedy decided that Kassem needed to go. Interestingly,
Kennedy received support from Britain and Israel but faced opposition from other allies, especially France and Germany.

Undeterred, Kennedy pressed on, and in 1962 the Central
Intelligence Agency set up a base of operations in Kuwait, fomented opposition to Kassem by supporting the anti-Communist
Baathist party, and armed Kurdish rebels under the code "Health
Alteration Committee." The CIA even sent Kassem a mono-
grammed poisoned handkerchief. On February 8, 1963, CIA-
backed conspirators staged a coup in Baghdad. Kassem held out
for a while but then surrendered. After a quick trial, he was shot
and his body shown on Iraqi television. Among the Baathist party
leaders who participated in the coup was the young Saddam Hussein, age twenty-five, who had fled Iraq for Egypt in 1958 after an
unsuccessful assassination attempt against Kassem.

The coup was accompanied by a bloodbath. The Baathists sys-
tematically murdered hundreds of the educated Iraqi elite, including doctors, lawyers, and teachers as well as military and political
figures. Soon infighting among the Baathist leadership broke out
as well. In 1968, another CIA-backed coup took place, this time
bringing to power Ahmed Hassan al-Bakr, a kinsman of Saddam
Hussein.

Despite these activities, the United States provided arms for
the new regime, and Western corporations such as Bechtel,
British Petroleum, and Mobil began doing business with Baghdad,
the first Western corporations to do so. These machinations took
place in the context of an overarching American policy goal to protect Israel and to promote governments in the region that would
allow oil to flow reliably to the West.

U.S. designs for the region were upset again in 1979 when the
Ayatollah Khomeini overthrew the Shah of Iran, who at the time
was America's closest ally in the Middle East, following Israel.
Khomeini set up a radical Islamic regime. In late 1979, Iranian
militants stormed the U.S. embassy in Tehran, took forty-three
American diplomats as hostage, and did not release them until
1981.

Looking for a counter to the Ayatollah, the United States and its European allies actively began to increase their support of Iraq, now led by Saddam Hussein, who had just replaced al-Bakr as head of the Baathist party and president of Iraq. Western support for Iraq included intelligence information, military equipment, and agricultural credits. The United States also deployed the largest naval force since the Vietnam War in the Persian Gulf. Ostensibly sent for the purpose of protecting oil tankers, it ended up engaging in attacks on Iran's navy. Washington encouraged and supported Iraq to wage war against the Iranians, which it did from 1979 to 1988. Ironically, it was Donald Rumsfeld, now secretary of defense, who in 1983 was sent by President Reagan as the American envoy to pave the way for the restoration of diplomatic relations with Iraq, which had been severed in 1967 as a result of the Six Day War between Israel and the Arab states.

The war with the Iranians initially went badly because Iran has a much larger population than Iraq and thus was able to field a much greater army. To compensate, the Americans suggested to the Iraqis that they use chemical agents. U.S. and British intelligence agents actually facilitated the Iraqi use of gas against the Iranians. Iraq then used poison gas against dozens of Kurdish villages in northern Iraq.

In 1985, the British company Uhde Ltd. built the Fulluja II plant fifty miles outside of Baghdad, which the Iraqis used for mustard and nerve gas production. The Thatcher government provided $21 million in financial backing through insurance guarantees. In addition, the Reagan administration eased up on its own technology export restrictions to Iraq, allowing the Iraqis to import supercomputers, machine tools, poisonous chemicals, and even strains of anthrax and bubonic plague. It should be noted that from 1986 to 1989, then–three star General Colin Powell served as the deputy national security advisor and then as national security advisor to President Reagan.

The United States and Britain helped arm Iraq with the very weapons of mass destruction that the second Bush administration and the Blair government were later to use as justification for forcibly removing Saddam from power. When Secretary of State Colin Powell offered proof of Saddam's chemical and biological weapons capacity to the U.N. Security Council in the months leading up to the Iraq war in 2003, he showed satellite photos of the Fulluja II plant. The American and the British governments were sure that Saddam had the chemical and biological weapons because they had helped secure them for him.

When the Iran-Iraq war ended in 1988, the United States continued to support Iraq, providing Saddam with military hardware, advanced technology, and agricultural credits. The United States looked to Saddam to maintain stability in the Persian Gulf. In August 1990, Saddam invaded Kuwait.

This sorry tale of Iraq is not an isolated incident. Unfortunately, similar accounts can be told of America propping up corrupt and authoritarian regimes around the world, including Pinochet in Chile, Samoza in Nicaragua, Noriega in Panama, Sukarno and Suharto in Indonesia, Marcos in the Philippines, apartheid governments in South Africa, King Faud in Saudi Arabia. The list is long and sordid.

During much of the Cold War, the U.S. government consistently placed interests over values, making unholy alliances with authoritarian regimes throughout Latin America, Africa, the Middle East, and Asia. These regimes were backed with massive armaments programs and propped up by U.S. policies and forces. This positioned the United States in world public opinion as fighting against human rights and democratic governance for the sake of national security considerations.

In exchange for military support and turning a blind eye to human rights abuses, American and other Western corporations received favored status in the exploitation of resources and labor. This created a situation in country after country in which America, the champion of democracy, became the defender of tyranny, and America, the supporter of free market economics, became the exploiter of the poor and the weak.

Backing authoritarian regimes led to an increasingly militarized American presence around the world. Successive American presidents spent less and less on cultural and humanitarian assistance and more and more on military sales and aid. During President Kennedy's administration, the United States spent only 1 percent of its GDP on promoting its influence overseas through the State Department, foreign aid, the United Nations, various information and cultural programs, and so on. This small percentage shrank under successive administrations until under George W. Bush, it was a mere 0.2 percent.

As Ignatieff puts it, "Even if you accept that generals can make good diplomats and special forces captains can make friends for the United States, it still remains true that the American presence overseas is increasingly armed, in uniform, and behind barbed wire and high walls. With every American embassy now hardened against terrorist attack, the empire's overseas outposts look increasingly like Fort Apache."[1]

Ignatieff makes the important observation: "This sort of projection of power, hunkered down against attack, can earn the United States fear and respect, but not admiration and affection. America's very strength—its military power—cannot conceal its weakness in the areas that really matter: the elements of power that do not subdue by force of arms but inspire by force of example."[2]

As American power has grown, American influence has diminished, leading to an increasing reliance on military power to further its interests. Ironically, no nation is planning to attack the United States on the front against which it is preparing the most, and it is neglecting leadership in those areas in which its leadership is most critically needed.

There is, of course, a deeply dialectical relationship between light and power. Empires may be motivated by a vision of democracy and freedom, but empires are not built by sweetness and light. They are built with armies and maintained by force. In the act of conquering the weak, the vision that initially motivated the empire is irreparably altered. In attaining power, the United States, like all empires before it, has had to make sacrifices and engage in trade-offs between its ideals and its interests. Otherwise, it would not have been able to traverse the distance between fledgling colonies, divided and weak, to imperial republic, united and strong, exercising global dominion.

The tragedy of empire is that in gaining it, democracy and the quest for social equity are often the first casualties. Power and freedom are invariably at odds with one another. The more power a nation acquires, the more freedom its citizens are called upon to surrender. This was the experience of Rome and Athens. Julius Caesar overthrew the Roman republic at the point when Rome had gained the Mediterranean world. After him, emperors, not democracy, ruled Rome. In Athens, overextension in fighting the Peloponnesian War brought Athens to its knees. After that, it faded from history as both empire and democracy. Great Britain was an exception. Parliamentary democracy continued to develop domestically in Britain during the eighteenth and nineteenth centuries, even as it was building its empire abroad.

The paradox is that if the United States had maintained absolute allegiance to the light by which it was founded, it would not have gained so much power. By gaining extraordinary power, it has lost a large measure of connection with the light. This raises the question of whether it is possible to use power for the sake of light. Can power serve light? Or is there something about power that inevitably diminishes the light?

During the Cold War, for example, the nuclear confrontation with the Soviet Union was so intense that democracy and human rights were consistently sacrificed in a struggle for the heart and soul of the world. Hence the U.S. support for the likes of Pinochet and the House of Saud. But finally, the Soviets fell. In attaining that victory, was ousting Allende, an avowed Marxist, and replacing him with Pinochet, an authoritarian general, a good thing or a bad thing, an act that kept communism from spreading in Latin America or a catalyst that drove people to anti-Americanism? Or was it both? Is backing a corrupt royal family in Saudi Arabia to ensure a predictable supply of oil a wise or an unwise decision? Should democratic institutions be sacrificed for commodities?

Will regime change in Iraq be the point of imperial overreach for the United States and ignite a new wave of terrorism? Or will a major U.S. presence in the Tigris-Euphrates river basin be the catalyst that brings democracy to the Middle East and peace between the Israelis and the Palestinians?

History guides in these matters but does not provide definitive answers. It is left to fallible leaders, acting with incomplete information and susceptible to hubris and the whims of prejudice, to make decisions and determine our fate. What Gibbon observed about the fall of Rome was that events almost always turned out completely differently than the actors themselves intended them to. This is what makes history so fascinating. It is the narrative of the complexity of the human soul: passionate, unpredictable, and entranced by the acquisition of knowledge for the exercise of greater power. This was the great temptation described in the Garden of Eden and about which Bacon wrote.

If we look back over time, the pattern we see is that whereas the quest for light provides the highest inspiration, the quest for power—as the ancient Hebrews understood—is the ultimate seduction. The drive for power emanates from the depths of the human psyche and soul, conjuring deep emotions and stirring complex feelings. The drive for power lies at the root of competitiveness. It is the impetus for knowledge. It is the goal of ambition. It is what compels us to violate the wisdom of limits.

One of the primary motivators for power is the sincere desire to do good, to manifest the light. This is what motivates our religious traditions. It is what motivates most of us most of the time. But the drive for power also has a shadow side. This is why the light is sacrificed so readily. The allure of power entices us to use dark means for the sake of enlightened ends. In so doing, we become corrupted, and both our ambitions and our motivations change so that we wish to use power simply for its own sake. This explains the close connection between power and force, which lies at the heart of empire.

Empires can sometimes rise to support the light, but they are always in the service of power. Empires invariably use force to maintain their dominion. When nations become empires, they generally become cynical about the light. The United States has not been nor will it be an exception. The world has already seen this in U.S. behavior during the Cold War, in the aftermath of 9/11, and in Iraq. As Lord Acton of Britain said famously in 1903, "Power corrupts, and absolute power corrupts absolutely."

The Transatlantic Relationship as a Cautionary Tale
All these complexities come into sharp relief in the current state of Euro-American relations, a point brilliantly made by policy analyst Robert Kagan in his book *Of Paradise and Power*. He points out:

On the all-important question of power—the efficacy of
power, the morality of power, the desirability of power—
American and European perspectives are diverging. Europe is
turning away from power . . . it is moving beyond power into a
self-contained world of laws and rules and transnational
negotiation and cooperation. . . . Meanwhile, the United
States remains mired in history, exercising power in the
anarchic Hobbesian world where international laws and rules
are unreliable and where true security and the defense and
promotion of a liberal order still depend on the possession and
use of military might.[3]

Empires by definition are essentially unbounded and constrained by no limits other than what they themselves impose or
which are implied by the limits of the power they can wield.
Empires may be glorious, but building and maintaining them is
also a messy, cruel, and dirty business. An imperium may have
control over others, but there is always someone out there determined to replace it, defy it, or undermine it. Of all political power
structures, the empire is simultaneously the most potent and the
most unstable.

Most European nations have already had their empires. Muse-
ums, art galleries, and statues across the length and breadth of
Europe detail their glories, agonies, victories, and defeats. The
unimaginable destruction of World Wars I and II, together with
the Holocaust, forced them, at least temporarily, to abandon the
imperial impulse. With the exception of the Russians, who maintained their imperial power until 1991, Europeans have come
together to form the European Union. Since World War II, they
have renegotiated national sovereignty in a community context
and have generally favored negotiation, diplomacy, and persuasion
over military force in settling differences. Europeans are now
quicker to appeal to international law, international public opinion, and international norms of conduct than to act unilaterally,
and they tend to view culture and commerce rather than military
supremacy and economic domination as the ties that bind nations
and peoples together.

In contrast, the United States is far less patient with diplomacy,
preferring coercive force and unilateral action, bolstered by ad

hoc "coalitions of the willing." Especially since 9/11, Americans
have been extremely sensitized to real or perceived threats and
have tended to divide the world into forces of good and evil, seeking finality and victory over the forces of darkness.

While Europe may seem cooperative and visionary today, its
history has been anything but benign. Europeans are responsible
for incredible bloodshed and violence both in Europe, and during
the era of its imperial reach around the world, in most of the rest
of the world. The United States, on the other hand, while today
definitely aggressive and unilateralist, was far less so for most of its
history, living for the most part far away from the cynical power
struggles of the Europeans and in fact serving as a haven for those
seeking escape from Europe's wars and cruelties.

Indeed, American diplomats of the eighteenth and nineteenth
centuries, while certainly pushing American interests forcefully
and with military backing, sounded very much like the European
diplomats of today. They argued for international norms and procedures rather than the use of brute force and extolled the utility
of commerce to bring peoples and nations together. The United
States certainly used force against its indigenous peoples, and the
force necessary to exert control over the Western Hemisphere and
to ensure the integrity of its markets, but when it came to dealing
with Europe it claimed the moral high ground and inveighed
against the cynical power mongering of European empires and
colonialism. As the weaker state, America was the principal propo-
nent of international law on the high seas during the eighteenth
century. The principal opponent was Great Britain, whose navy
was then "Mistress of the Seas."

Two centuries later, the Europeans and the Americans have
traded places and perspectives, but they have not done so because
the Europeans have somehow become more moral and the Americans less so. They have traded places simply because the power
equation has been inverted: the stronger has become the weaker,
and the weaker has become the stronger. When Europe was
strong, it glorified military might and reveled in the superiority of
its power. Now it is militarily weak and extols the virtues of international law and the need to honor diversity. When the United

States was weak, it practiced the politics of discretion and modesty. Now it is strong and behaves as empires always have: as the biggest bully on the block.

When the Cold War ended, this disparity between Europe and America became obvious. Instead of viewing the collapse of the Soviet Union as an opportunity to demonstrate that a united Europe could be a superpower in its own right, the Europeans sought to enjoy a peace dividend. Defense budgets across Europe dropped to less than 2 percent of GDP, and even military operations in Europe—Kosovo being the prime example—were accomplished only with U.S. help.

The end of the Cold War had the opposite effect on the United States. There was no peace dividend for America. Almost immediately after the fall of the Berlin Wall, Saddam Hussein invaded Kuwait, prompting the largest American military action since Vietnam, in which the Europeans played an important political but minor military role. The Gulf War demonstrated that, with the demise of the Soviet Union, American military power could be deployed with impunity anywhere in the world. This was the moment when the United States definitively succeeded Great Britain as the world's leading empire.

This unipolar moment had a predictable consequence: American military power, now unchallenged, began to be used more frequently and unilaterally. President Bush, Sr., deployed troops in Panama in 1989, in the Gulf War in 1991, and in Somalia, a humanitarian intervention, in 1992. President Clinton took military action in Haiti in 1993, Somalia in 1995, Bosnia in 1996, and Kosovo in 1999. Although both presidents spoke eloquently of pulling back in the aftermath of the Cold War, in fact American might began to be deployed abroad with greater frequency and decisiveness and with no real military opposition. President George W. Bush forced regime change in Afghanistan in 2001 and invaded Iraq in 2003.

Power begets power and the desire to use that power. If someone is at home and observes a prowler outside, that person will have a much more cautious reaction if he is unarmed. The normal reaction would be to call the police, who have the force necessary to deal with the situation. But if the homeowner has a gun, he or she may be much more bold in confronting the intruder. How much power we possesses or have access to determines the range of possible responses to danger or threat and the willingness to use them.

This difference in possession and perception of power played itself out in the situation in Iraq. Most Europeans were bewildered and stubbornly resistant in the face of Washington's insistence that regime change was necessary. For Europeans, the risks involved in removing Saddam Hussein were greater than the risks of containing him. They were like the homeowner without a gun. Americans, on the other hand, stronger and traumatized by 9/11, had a much lower threshold to the perception of threat. They also had the power to do something about it. Americans were like the homeowner with a gun as well as being the police. Although there was no practical possibility of Europeans doing anything about Saddam Hussein, for Americans, especially having just accomplished regime change in Afghanistan with relative ease, dealing with Iraq seemed eminently practicable and in fact necessary for national security and global stability.

These different perceptions are not simply psychological. As weaker states, Europeans are not nearly as threatened by rogue states as is the United States. A century ago when Europeans were in their imperial phase and America was weak, what happened in Africa, the Middle East, and Asia was of acute concern to the Europeans, and especially to the British. In contrast, the events were of only marginal concern to the Americans, except for specific threats to commerce.

Now the situation—like the power equation—is reversed. From the point of view of strategic planning and setting political priorities, neither Iraq nor Iran nor North Korea—President Bush's Axis of Evil—amount to much for the Europeans. Even China, considered militarily, is not thought of as a European problem. Both Europeans and Americans agree that these are principally American problems.

If you look a little deeper at this disparity in power, and the difference in perception and practicality that being an empire makes, you could say that Europeans can afford to be as benign and tolerant as they are precisely because the United States protects them. They have the opportunity to forego power politics at the world level precisely because the United States does not.

Supported by the United States, the Europeans have been able to develop what British diplomat Robert Cooper calls a "postmodern state" that no longer rests on the balance of power but on the "rejection of force" combined with "self-enforced rules of behavior." In the postmodern world, says Cooper, "the amorality of Machiavelli's theories of statecraft . . . have been replaced by a moral consciousness in international affairs."[4]

This miracle of history came from the realization that the European shadow side, represented so dramatically and malignantly by the Nazis, must never be allowed to manifest itself again. In this sense, the commitment to form the European Union and the concomitant rejection of the use of force inside European borders is a European attempt to block any resurgence of its German shadow side and its "will to power." This represents an achievement without equal in modern times, for which the Europeans are to be commended. Never before in history have so many warring nations come together at so many levels to form so durable a peace. What they have wrought is a harbinger of the new world order about which humankind has forever dreamed.

But again, it is also an achievement that would not have occurred if the United States was not willing to remain precisely in the world that the Europeans were leaving: the world of anarchy, treachery, cynicism, and brute force, the breeding ground for empire. The Europeans have been able to share their houses peacefully with each other because the Americans have the guns and play the policeman, protecting the Europeans from intruders such as the Soviet Union during the Cold War and even assisting them in settling their internal squabbles when these squabbles got bloody, as happened in Kosovo.

It was the United States that rebuilt Europe through the Marshall Plan and established and led the NATO alliance against the Soviet Union, behind which Europe prospered. It was the United States that maintained garrisons of hundreds of thousands of troops and bases in Europe and around the world to keep the peace and even led European forces into battles dealing, as in Kosovo, with exclusively European problems. It was the United States that ensured that Germany did not rise again and threaten European stability. And it was the United States that took the leadership in creating the United Nations and Bretton Woods institutions, which fashioned the international order that has governed human affairs and commerce for the past sixty years, in which Europeans have played central roles.

In effect, the Americans extended the Monroe Doctrine to Europe, declaring that in addition to the Western Hemisphere, Europe was also off-limits to foreign powers. Behind this shield, Europeans were able to leave war behind and prosper.

This is a crucial point in understanding the complexity of empire and the heavy responsibility an empire has in ordering its priorities and interests. American support of the rebuilding of Europe after the Second World War is an extraordinary example of empire at its best and one of the most impressive examples of the effective use of national sovereignty in all of human history. But this achievement only came after the European descent into the madness of nazism and bolshevism, so that the United States, quite literally on behalf of the entire world community, including Europe, said, "Never again." The apogee point of the American application of *constructive* power came at the nadir point of the European *corruption* of power.

The paradox in this, says Kagan, is that "although the United States has played the critical role in bringing Europe into this Kantian paradise, it cannot enter the paradise itself. It mans the walls but cannot enter the gate. The United States, with all its vast power, remains stuck in history, left to deal with the Saddams and the ayatollahs, the Kim Jong Ils and Jiang Zemins, leaving most of the benefits to others."[5]

HUBRIS AND THE WISDOM OF LIMITS   In both the American ascent to empire and the European descent to regionalism, we can see the contradictory effect of empire and the crucial need for empires to learn the wisdom of limits. Because the Europeans did not learn these limits, they forfeited their power and even today are afraid of any German resurgence. The wisdom of limits is something the Americans must learn if they are to have any hope of sustaining the power they have now gained. It is when limits can be violated that they are the most badly needed. But, paradoxically, it is precisely its power that gives the United States the capacity to violate limits. Yet if they are not self-imposed, they will be compelled, sooner or later, by either internal or external forces, and generally in a tragic and destructive way.

Recent European history provides an exquisite example of this timeless truth. At the apex of European imperial power, Hitler's madness did not seem even remotely conceivable. If we go back a little more than a hundred years to the last quarter of the nineteenth century, the European powers had circumnavigated the globe and consolidated imperial power, quite literally, over most of the peoples of Africa and Asia. Moreover, between 1878 and 1890, there had been seven crucial inventions, almost all of which were developed in the United States, that made modernity possible: electricity, the telephone, the car, the subway, the elevator, steel-frame skyscrapers, and mass transit. Together these inventions, combined with European imperialism, brought the industrial revolution to a feverish pitch of productivity and innovation, generating unprecedented prosperity, and for the first time, global finance, global communication, and global trade. It was the world's first experience of globalization.

At the Paris Exhibition in 1900, where Europe came together to celebrate the new century, there was exuberant rhetoric about the fact that free trade would soon dominate the world and make it safe for Western-style democracy. People believed that war would soon be essentially obsolete, as scientific rationalism, democratic capitalism, and Western civilization continued to flourish in Europe and were carried by European armies, missionaries, and traders to all conquered lands. Those were heady days for the West.

Europeans were so confident that few noticed when a minor duke was assassinated in August 1914 in Sarajevo. Even after the carnage of the First World War, President Wilson declared that it had been the war to end all wars, almost as if the Great War itself had been a small aberration in the inevitable march of progress in which everyone so deeply believed.

But there was no march of progress. Within less than a decade after the armistice, Adolf Hitler had been democratically elected chancellor of Germany and began his relentless march for empire, a Reich that was intended to last a thousand years. Then came the Second World War, the Holocaust, nuclear weapons, and the Cold War, from which the world is only just beginning to emerge. The United States was and is the crucial factor in the world's collective emergence from the madness that gripped Europe at the collapse of its imperial dynasties and in the new world order that was established after the Second World War. But it must know that imperiums die hard, and they are immune neither to external threats nor to the internal blindness that the hubris of empire breeds.

These truths may seem moralistic because American power seems so invincible. But they emanate from deep history, from the depths of human experience over millennia. They constitute the breeding ground that creates empire, challenges empire, and ultimately, defeats empire. The American empire will not be an exception. It has risen and is now at or near its zenith. The only real question is how long it will last before it dissolves away or falls.

6

The Rise and Fall of Empires

IN LOOKING BACK AT THE IMPERIAL ACTIVITIES and attitudes of the ancient Greeks or Romans, Chinese or Muslims, we find the same imperial impulse that now grips America. There are the same issues of light and power, the same appetite to conquer land, populations, and resources, and the same ambitions, rivalries, virtues, and vices that make each empire both a replica of the same pattern and yet a drama all its own.

THE BEGINNINGS OF EMPIRE The earliest empires arose in what is called the Fertile Crescent, framed by the alluvial plains of the Tigris-Euphrates river basin. These rivers are thousands of miles long, originating in what is now Turkey and running parallel to one another until they empty as one river into the Persian Gulf. These majestic rivers enabled both commerce and travel over long distances. Their annual flooding, particularly the Euphrates, provided rich agricultural land. It was along the northern reaches of the Euphrates, in Syria-Palestine, that the Neolithic revolution began some ten thousand years ago, and humankind began the process of domesticating plants and animals.

During the Neolithic revolution, time and life quickened along the eastern Mediterranean. The quantitative developments of the tens of thousands of years of the earlier Paleolithic, hunter-gatherer culture, led to qualitative shifts in technology, social functioning, and religious cosmology. When people began actually planting grains, probably somewhere along the upper reaches of the Euphrates River, food gathering was transformed into gardening, and eventually, into agriculture. Humankind took "nature into culture," to use the phrase of social philosopher William Irwin Thompson, and developed a source of food hundreds of times more plentiful than was possible through hunting or simple foraging.

With this advance into predictable plentitude, pottery was developed to hold the grains that had to be stored. Pottery was also useful in carrying grains and other items to neighboring settlements, because with agriculture came trade. Men still hunted, of course, as they had for some three million years since they descended from the trees in eastern Africa. But with the transformation of food gathering into food cultivation, hunting ceased to be critical for the survival of the group. It became instead what it has been ever since: a ritualized activity important for male bonding and for strengthening a sense of masculinity.

The hunter-gatherers had little or no property, and there is little evidence of them trading. They moved self-sufficiently with the herds, which they used for food as needed. Agriculture brought about a more sedentary existence, with fields and storage sites that required protection. For the first time the bow and arrow and the spear were needed not for hunting but for the protection of land. The development of agriculture was followed by the development of the art of combat. Rituals of the hunt were transformed into campaigns of war.

The period from 9000 to 7000 B.C. was one of momentous transformation in human affairs. By 6500 B.C., agriculture, property, and trade flourished throughout the entire Tigris-Euphrates river basin, and various city-states and kingdoms had developed. There were incessant wars as well. It was here, somewhere around 4000 B.C., that the first civilization arose. Cultural historians and anthropologists generally point to irrigation farming, writing, and technical specialization as the practical developments that allowed civilization to emerge. The epicenter of this first experience of civilization was Sumer, on the alluvial plains between the Tigris and Euphrates rivers in what is now central Iraq.

With the first civilization came the first empire, associated with a Sumerian king called Sargon I who lived from 2334 to 2279 B.C. As part of the first civilization and the founder of the first empire, Sargon is one of the most important people to have ever lived. A monolith unearthed in an archeological dig about one hundred years ago near the ancient Persian city of Susa depicts Sargon adorned with a majestic tailored beard and dressed in the robes of a sovereign. Cuneiform tablets, expressing the first written language, describe his birth by saying: "My humble mother conceived me; in secret she brought me forth. She placed me in a basket-boat of rushes; with pitch she closed my door."[1] Set adrift in the mighty Euphrates, Sargon was rescued by a peasant and taken to the king who took him in. Sargon eventually became the king's cupbearer. This narrative predates a strikingly similar story about Moses by over a thousand years.

Eventually, Sargon overthrew the king and mounted the throne of the city-state of Akkad, proclaiming himself King of Universal Dominion. He is remembered as "Sargon the Great" by historians because he pillaged numerous cities, slaughtered many people, and knit together the world's first recorded empire, encompassing much of the land from the Persian Gulf north between the Tigris and Euphrates rivers and west to the Mediterranean Sea.

When Sargon reached the Persian Gulf, he waded out into the sea, and before his entire army, washed his weapons in symbolic triumph over his enemies. Fierce, despotic, and cruel, Sargon reigned with a military rod of iron for fifty-five years. When he died, the entire empire rose in revolt but was quelled by his three sons who succeeded him.

Sargon's successors held imperial sway for another two centuries until the Sumerian Empire dissipated into chaos and warfare and was supplanted by the youthful and dynamic Babylonian Empire, originating farther north up the Euphrates. History's second empire was established by the mighty Hammurabi, who lived from 2123 to 2081 B.C. Babylonia was an amalgam of the Sumerians and Akkadians with a new capital at Babylon, sixty miles south of present-day Baghdad.

While Sargon ruled by the sword and the fist, Hammurabi ruled by the sword and the scales. Under him, the petty warring city-states of Mesopotamia were forged into unity, disciplined into order, and provided security through the application of a historic code of laws known as the Code of Hammurabi. By analyzing the revolt that was the legacy of Sargon, Hammurabi learned the most important lesson of empire: longevity is based on the fair application of law. Thus the prologue to his code states:

> When the lofty Anu, King of the Annunaki and Bel, Lord of Heaven and Earth . . . pronounced the lofty name of Babylon, when they made it famous among the quarters of the world and in its midst established an everlasting kingdom . . . Anu and Bel called me, Hammurabi . . . to cause justice to prevail in the land, to destroy the wicked and the evil, to prevent the strong from oppressing the weak . . . to enlighten the land and to further the welfare of the people.[2]

The 285 laws that were contained in the code were scientifically divided into categories, ranging from business regulations, compensation for injuries, family affairs, labor laws, property rights, and capital and noncapital punishments. Due mainly to the institution of these laws, which united the empire, Hammurabi died peacefully, and the empire of Babylonia lasted more than four hundred years.

After the Babylonians, the empire of the warlike Assyrians, reminiscent of Sargon, arose farther north along the Tigris from their capital of Ninevah, and the epic tale of empires began. What is essential for our purposes here is a point made by the historian Irwin St. John Tucker: "When the misty curtain first parts for us upon that stage whereon the drama of life is played, emperors occupy the center of the scene. They have held the leading role ever since."[3]

It is at the inception of human civilization that we find the genesis of empire. There, at the beginning, we find all the issues with which the United States is grappling today. From the earliest days of Sumer, all the complexities of power and light were set forth, particularly the choice between empire by sword and force or empire by sword and law. Sargon in the third millennium B.C. and Bush in the third millennium A.D. grappled with same deep questions concerning power for the sake of power or power for the sake of light.

Durant makes the additional point that "civilization, like life, is a perpetual struggle with death. And as life maintains itself only by abandoning the old, and recasting itself in younger and fresher forms, so civilization achieves a precarious survival by changing habitat or its blood. It moved from Ur to Babylon and Judea, from Babylon to Ninevah, from these to Persepolis, Sardis, and Miletus, and from these, Egypt and Crete to Greece and Rome."[4] As civilizations shifted, so did empires.

CHARACTERISTICS OF EMPIRE   One characteristic common to all empires without exception is that they involve core and peripheral territories. There is always a dominant state and subordinate states. The Sumerian, Babylonian, and Assyrian empires were centered in the Fertile Crescent in the cities of Akkad, Babylon, and Ninevah, respectively. Their subordinate territories extended generally from the Persian Gulf north and westward toward the Mediterranean Sea. The Persian Empire arose to the east and was centered around Persepolis, reaching up into what is now Iran. The Roman Empire was centered in Italy with its capital in Rome, and its territories ringed the Mediterranean Sea.

The French, British, Dutch, Spanish, and Portuguese empires of the eighteenth and nineteenth centuries were all run from their respective European capitals and comprised far-flung colonial holdings in North and South America, Africa, the Middle East, and Asia. There was a time when the sun literally never set on the British Empire, such was the expanse of its colonial holdings, yet all of them were governed from London.

There have been continuous empires, such as the Roman Empire, where Italy dominated both the land and the sea within the Mediterranean region, as well as adjacent lands, but in which the entire empire was more or less a single unit. There have been discontinuous empires, such as the British Empire, where Britain dominated lands far from British shores. There are also empires that combine both, such as the German Reich with imperial possessions adjacent to Germany as well as possessions in Africa and Asia.

Empires can exercise formal power, such as the Soviet empire did over eastern Europe, where the control was direct, hierarchical, and clear. Empires may also exercise informal control, such as the United States does over Latin America through the Monroe Doctrine or over any number of nations in the global south through the International Monetary Fund and the World Bank. While formal control is direct and often harshly enforced, informal control is generally more subtle and exercised more often through threat and intermediary institutions, often simply through financial and political manipulation. American imperial power is virtually always applied through informal means, reinforced by military action when informal means are deemed insufficient. As with all definitions, the dividing line between continuous and discontinuous, and formal and informal empires is often blurred and inexact. But it helps in understanding some of the techniques and behavioral forms that empires take over subordinate societies and lands.

American power in Afghanistan began very formally in the sense that U.S. and allied troops were involved, but it has now shifted to increasingly informal control as Afghanistan develops its own internal structures of governance. Similarly with Iraq. Would Afghanistan and Iraq be considered a formal part of a U.S. empire? No. Are their governments under U.S. control? Absolutely. Whatever the modality and method, the core elites, in this case Washington over Afghanistan and Iraq, exercise authority and control over subordinate countries and societies in terms of the structure of their economy, design of their government, disposal of their resources, and orientation of their defense and foreign policies. Such control is the means and end of empire.

In the overseas empires of the British, Dutch, Germans, Spanish, and Portuguese, natural resources were extracted from the colonies and shipped back to Europe. Manufactured goods from

Europe were shipped to the colonies. There were also triangular arrangements, such as the slave trade, whereby manufactured goods were sent from Europe to Africa, slaves were sent from Africa to the colonies in North and South America, and raw materials were sent from the Americas to Europe. In this sense, empires resemble gigantic machines or organisms with interlocking parts arranged so as to benefit the dominant state and culture. Maintaining such structures over time was and continues to be a high art form.

The Roman Empire endured the longest of any in human history: more than a thousand years through Byzantium and about five hundred in the West. The Babylonians, Assyrians, Hapsburgs, Russians, and Ottomans lasted for about four hundred years each. The Sumerian, Persian, Mongol, French, British, and Dutch empires lasted for about two hundred. The Soviet empire collapsed after about seventy years, and the Nazis flamed out after twelve, setting the record for both cruelty and brevity.

The Arab caliphate took about one hundred years to reach its zenith in 700 A.D. and then another two hundred to decline. The Mongols burst into history around 1200, expanded dramatically over the next hundred years, and then rapidly declined, fading away completely by around 1400. The Ming dynasty in China grew from around 1350 to around 1450 and then declined over the next two centuries. The Ottoman Empire grew from the 1350s to the 1550s, then remained at its zenith for a full three hundred years before declining during the later part of the 1800s, finally succumbing to the European powers in World War I. The British and the French empires expanded dramatically from 1750 to 1800, reached their peak by 1900, and then lost virtually everything in the aftermath of World War II.

THE RISE AND FALL OF EMPIRES   Imperial beginnings are marked by decisive leadership, clear objectives, the willingness to use force to gain strategic ends, and an *esprit de corps* that motivates the dominant nation to spill over its borders for land, resources, and control. The conquests of Alexander the Great provide the classic example of an empire formed by the charisma of a military leader; Alexander swept out of Greece and over Persia at the age of eighteen by the sheer force of personality and military genius. Genghis Khan is another example, sweeping out of Mongolia in 1206 to establish the largest empire in history, which at its zenith covered two-thirds of the Eurasian landmass. Military historians consider the Khan the father of modern warfare and one of the greatest military tacticians in the history of war. Napoleon provides a more contemporary example of an emperor who extended territory by a combination of military brilliance and the *esprit de corps* of an army, in his case inspired by the ideals of the French Revolution.

Expanding empires generally possess superior military technology, greater social differentiation, and deeper institutional cohesiveness than the nations they conquer. In the case of Alexander, it was his refinement of the phalanx and tactical maneuvering. With Genghis Khan, it was his extraordinary use of the horse. As for Napoleon, his innovations in artillery were key to his success.

When the British, French, Portuguese, and Spanish came to the Western Hemisphere during the sixteenth and seventeenth centuries, they found indigenous peoples without any kind of firearm technology. There were no animals in the Western Hemisphere, such as horses or camels, that were capable of carrying a soldier into battle. Nor did the native peoples have the technology to build oceangoing ships. As a result, the Incas in Peru, the Aztecs in Mexico, the Iroquois in North America, among numerous other tribes, were easily and quickly overcome by relatively small groups of invaders. The Europeans had similar victories when they colonized Africa and Asia. Western technology, especially in the weapons of war, was so superior to anything it encountered that victory was virtually inevitable everywhere European traders and armies went.

Empires also can be ignited by a dynamic ideology. The Arab expansion of the seventh century was catalyzed by Muhammad and the genesis of Islam. When the Arab armies spilled north out of Arabia after Muhammad's death, they found the Persian Empire to the northeast and Byzantine Empire to the northwest in decline, unable to mobilize effective opposition. Within less than a hundred years, Arab armies conquered lands stretching from the Pyrenees in Spain to the Indus River in India, carrying the new teachings of Islam. Only when they sought to penetrate the heart of Europe itself was their western expansion halted.

This is not to say that empires are carefully thought through and organized. Alexander the Great knew where he was going and was certain that his purpose was to spread Greek culture to the Persian Empire. Genghis Khan believed his destiny was to rule the world. But most empires evolve much more slowly and opportunistically, almost haphazardly. As the British historian J. R. Seeley observed of the British in 1883, at the height of their imperial power, "We seem to have conquered and peopled half the world in a fit of absence of mind."[5] The acquisition of power, like its dissolution, seems to be largely unpremeditated, which from a historical point of view makes it all the more predictable.

Empires decay and implode or are, in turn, challenged and conquered by an emerging power in much the same way that they emerged. Indeed, it is generally an internal decay, coming together with an external challenge, that initiates the end of an empire. When an expanding power meets a decaying one, it conquers; when it succumbs to decay, it is conquered. As Durant puts it, "It is almost a law of history that the same wealth that generates a civilization announces its decay. For wealth produces ease as well as art; it softens a people to the ways of luxury and peace, and invites invasion from stronger arms and hungrier mouths."[6]

ATHENS

The genius of Athenian democracy has already been discussed. What needs to be chronicled here is its tragic experience of empire, a tale that the United States in particular should note. It may be that democracies do not good empires make.

After the victory of the Greeks over the Persians at the battle of Salamis in 480 B.C., Athens consolidated its hegemony among the Greek city-states and in 466 B.C. led the Greeks to final victory over the Persians in the battle of Eurymedon. Athens experienced something similar to what the Americans experienced during and after World War II. The enemy was so ferocious and Athens so noble in its victory, that most of the Greek city-states, Sparta being an important exception, embraced Athenian leadership. Then in its golden age, Athenian democracy was considered the light of all Greece. Accepting this leadership, Athens decided which of the states should send money, which ones should send ships, and who should lead the troops into battle.

What was initially an alliance was transformed into an empire when Athens and the Delian League of Greek city-states that it led began to capture cities, enslave populations, and colonize lands. Then Athens began to intimidate the Delian League itself, forcing the member cities to provide troops and money for its wars of conquest. Athens sent out emissaries to exact tribute and supervise the policies of the weaker cities. The Delian League thus became an empire through which Athens exerted political control, largely by informal means, but reinforced by military threat.

So blatant and aggressive were the Athenians in their imperial rule that much of Greece rallied around Sparta, a highly militarized and authoritarian city-state, to form a counteralliance called the Peloponnesian League. As effective on land as Athens was at sea, Sparta led its forces against Athens and finally defeated it in the Peloponnesian War. All of Greece was left devastated, even the victors. The irony was that Athens, the leading democracy, created such oppressive conditions that Sparta, the harshest authoritarian state, led the rebellion for freedom against it.

Like America today, Athens was widely popular for its democracy but deeply resented because of the undemocratic means it used to gain and maintain imperial power. As Thucydides recounts, Athens was an "education to Greece" but was also feared and hated. In acquiring power, Athens denied others the very democratic principles it had pioneered at home and for which it was heralded throughout the Mediterranean world.

The imperial arc of Athens was short-lived. The Athenian Empire was fully in place by 445 B.C. and had collapsed by 405 B.C. It was remarkably turbulent and unstable, with frequent rebellions and defections. The Athenian Empire provides a classic case of overreach, deciding for political and economic reasons to invade and colonize Sicily after consolidating imperial control in

Greece over the Delian League. Expedition after expedition was sent, only to meet defeat after defeat. Vast sums of money were expended, but to little effect. Finally, the Athenians withdrew.

Athens also succumbed to the erosion of internal dissent and political turbulence. Democracy was its greatest strength and its greatest weakness. A state that responds to the popular will draws forth from its citizens both the highest of human ideals and the basest of human impulses. Thus, at the same time Socrates was conducting his dialogues about truth, beauty, and goodness, Athens was fighting the Peloponnesian War and trying to colonize Sicily.

As the war dragged on, deprivation and suffering increased, leading to social unrest and political dissention. Demagogues emerged, and the unity required for dominance dissipated away. It was at the hands of the demagogues that Socrates was forced to drink the hemlock. Different Athenian factions competed for the allegiance of the different fleets and armies scattered across the empire until there was no longer the internal cohesion required to withstand the disciplined Spartan attacks. Thucydides said it best: "In the end, it was only because they had destroyed themselves by their own internal strife that finally they were forced to surrender."[7]

ROME

Legend has it that Aeneas, fleeing the destruction of Troy at the hands of the Greeks, founded Rome. It was built on one of seven hills on the banks of the Tiber River during the eighth century B.C. From the beginning, its people and leaders were inspired by a prophetic vision that one day Rome would rule the world. Slowly, incrementally, inexorably, Rome expanded to dominate its neighbors. By the third century B.C., it had control over all of Italy.

In 265 B.C. Rome came into open conflict with Carthage, an equally powerful city-state, which dominated the eastern Mediterranean from its capital on the coast of North Africa in what is present-day Libya. The First Punic War between the two superpowers of the Mediterranean was for control of Sicily. Rome won, establishing dominion over the island, and the Carthaginians retreated to Carthage. Carthage counterattacked under the famous Hannibal in the late third century in the Second Punic War. This time, the Roman victory was decisive. In the Third Punic War, initiated by the Romans, Carthage was utterly destroyed, and the city was leveled and sown with salt.

Like the United States after the collapse of the Soviet Union, Rome then emerged as a power without peer. It moved quickly to defeat Macedonia, which had sided with Carthage, and from there slowly asserted control over Greece and Palestine, establishing complete dominion over the entire Mediterranean world by 133 B.C.

Edward Gibbon, whose classic *History of the Decline and Fall of the Roman Empire* was published the same year that the American Revolution began, believed that Rome rose to empire because of the national patriotism of its people, the effectiveness of its legions, and the strength of its government. It ranks as perhaps the greatest empire ever built because it brought together social and religious cohesion, technical and organizational capacity, and political and institutional solidity. Rome was quintessentially political, conquering through massive military might but enforcing unity through the application of law.

A Roman historian of the time, Polybius, contrasted the economic imperialism of Carthage with what he described as the cultural and social forces driving Rome. Above all, he said, Romans demonstrated fidelity, honor, and faith. Like Americans, the Romans were deeply convinced of their manifest destiny. This made the Romans self-confident, fearless, and "impatient in repose," as Polybius put it. The drive to greatness imbued the people with hope in every crisis, empowered the legions as they went out to conquer, and inspired the government to maintain a long-term strategic focus in the face of adversity.

Rome fell primarily because it overextended its borders and did not fully appreciate the strength of the Germanic tribes to the north. Gibbon describes how the emperor Augustus—who reigned from 31 B.C. to 14 A.D. and restored the greatness of Rome after the disintegration of the republic and the assassination of Julius Caesar—advised his successors in his last will and testament to maintain an empire "within those limits which Nature seemed to have placed as its permanent bulwarks and boundaries: on the west the Atlantic Ocean; the Rhine and Danube on the north; the Euphrates on the east; and towards the south the sandy deserts of Arabia and Africa."[8] Inside these boundaries was the civilized world; beyond them lived the barbarians.

The "vanity and ignorance" of the Romans, writes Gibbon, lay in their thinking that the lands beyond their imperial borders were unimportant. As he puts it, Rome fell because its leaders made the fatal mistake of "confounding the Roman monarchy with the globe of the earth." Hubris was at the core of the fall of the mighty Romans. "The decline of Rome," he adds, "was the natural and inevitable effect of immoderate greatness. Prosperity ripened the principle of decay; the causes of destruction multiplied with the extent of conquest; and as soon as time or accident had removed the artificial supports, the stupendous fabric yielded to the pressure of its own weight."[9]

Gibbon goes on to describe how, during the first and second centuries A.D., the Roman army and the bureaucracy grew to become enormous semiautonomous organizations, while wealth and property became increasingly concentrated in the hands of fewer and fewer landlords and aristocrats, who specialized in tax avoidance and strategies to protect their families and vassals from becoming recruits in the emperor's army.

Add to this the growing independent power of the Church beginning in the third century A.D., and the emperors found themselves increasingly unable to govern effectively. When the state sought resources or recruits, it had to make concessions to the rich, who increasingly ruled with semifeudal power. In the end, this vicious cycle of tax evasion and privatization left the central government impoverished, the rich fewer and wealthier, and the mass of people destitute and dependent on state welfare to survive. Does any of this sound familiar?

The decline took on alarming proportions in the third century, when rebellious frontier troops routinely placed their commanders on the imperial throne. Seeing this weakness, barbarians attacked from northern and eastern Europe, and the Persians sought to reconquer Mesopotamia. The emperor Aurelius stabilized the situation when he defeated the Goths in 268–269, withdrew Roman troops from Dacia, and redeployed Roman legions in Egypt and Gaul. Diocletian and Constantine reformed both the army and the bureaucracy but did not solve the underlying structural, political, and economic problems. In fact, Constantine's relocation of the imperial capital from Rome to Constantinople in 330 diminished Rome's stature and strengthened the independent power of the aristocracy and military commanders in the western half of the empire.

Meanwhile, the vaunted Roman legions continued to attract more and more barbarians; Rome allowed this to happen partly in order to ensure recruits, and partly in order to appease potential invaders. But the result was only increased civil unrest and military instability. After marauding for decades, the Vandals finally overran Gaul in 406–407; the Visigoths invaded Italy and sacked Rome in 410; Attila the Hun wreaked havoc in the Danube provinces between 433 and 453; the Vandals reached and captured Carthage in 439; and the Osigoths occupied Pannonia in 454. At this point, the western part of the Roman Empire completely disintegrated and Europe descended into the Dark Ages.

Such was the strength of Roman institutions and the capabilities of a succession of emperors that the eastern part of the empire survived for another thousand years, keeping stability throughout the Aegean, the Balkans, and Asia Minor. Byzantium reached its zenith in the sixth and seventh centuries A.D., after which came a long period of imperial decline.

Byzantium fell for reasons very similar to its western counterpart: its emperors grew increasingly unable to control bloated bureaucracies or feudal aristocracies, suffering the whims of the military and the machinations of nobles and courtiers. State treasuries were diminished as the aristocracy gained more and more tax exemptions. Meanwhile, the emperors clung to the Byzantian tradition of opulence and magnificence of display and compensated for diminished budgets by allowing the navy and strategic fortresses to fall into decay.

THE OTTOMANS

The Seljuk Turks seized most of Asia Minor during the late thir-teenth century, and the Christian Crusades emanating from Europe—especially the fourth, led by the Venetians—destroyed institutions established by Diocletian and Constantine and shat-tered the tradition of unified government in the Aegean, which dated back to the Roman republic. The Balkans were lost during the fourteenth century, and finally, in 1451, Constantinople fell to the Ottomans.

The Ottomans consolidated control over what was left of Byzantium and expanded north into the Balkans, east into the Fer-tile Crescent, and south into Arabia, reaching their apex in the six-teenth and seventeenth centuries. During the eighteenth century, Ottoman power seemed solid but internal decay was apparent. The central government became bloated and ineffective, increas-ingly leaving local control to rapacious landlords and military com-manders. Military and technological modernization was subordinated to lavish expenditures by the court, and civil strife among the conquered peoples broke out.

Tax avoidance by the rich, the bane of all empires, was again a critical problem. In the case of the Ottomans, it was so effective that fully two-thirds of the government's budget was supplied by tithes and livestock taxes on the peasants. In fact, the wealthy prof-ited enormously as tax collectors. But peasant taxes do not an empire make, and the central government was challenged with covering state expenditures in the face of an increasing mountain of debt.

Meanwhile, the European powers were bursting with energy. They sailed worldwide on their modern ships, fighting with mod-ern weaponry and eagerly seeking raw materials for the factories that the industrial revolution made possible. Russia took the terri-tories north of the Black Sea and Crimea from the Ottomans dur-ing the eighteenth century. The expanding Hapsburg Empire took Hungary and parts of Serbia and Wallachia, and Iran began to exert pressure from the east. The Serbs rebelled in 1804 and again in 1815. The Greeks fought a war of independence from 1822 to

1830, and Britain, France, Russia, and Austria seized substantial portions of northern Africa and the Balkans.

The crowning blow against the Ottomans came in 1873, when the Congress of Berlin partitioned Bulgaria; granted Serbia, Romania, and Montenegro their independence; gave Tunisia to France; and handed Cyprus over to Britain. The Ottomans were too weakened and corrupt to resist effectively, but they carried into World War I the deep antagonisms caused by centuries of erosion and conflict with the Europeans. They wrongly sided with the Germans against the British and the French and saw the complete dismemberment of their empire, the creation of Turkey as a modern state, and most of the Middle East turned into British and French protectorates, including Palestine, under British rule.

THE EUROPEANS

The Europeans, particularly the British, now held imperial sway. But they were to perpetuate and succumb to the same imperial pattern of enlargement, decay, and dissolution. Indeed, a century and a half earlier, the American colonies had successfully rebelled for the same reasons that colonies all over the world and throughout history have rebelled: the failure of the center to establish full bureaucratic control over the periphery.

The fall of the Spanish Empire was classic in this regard. As with Rome, colonial landholdings were either given to or sold to imperial or local aristocrats and military commanders as rewards for individual good service or to obtain revenues or recruits. But these vast landholdings eventually turned into semiautonomous fiefdoms a very long way from the imperial core.

Because of this independence, imperial control began to mean little more than collecting taxes, something any local region would resent and eventually resist, especially if it was half a world away, as Latin America was from Madrid. When many of the colonies— Venezuela, Argentina, and Cuba in particular—developed dynamic economies, while at the same time the economy of Spain was declining, the colonial elites, caught between loyalty to Spain and the prospect of revolt by the locals, had to make some tough decisions.

The Thirty Years' War, 1618 to 1648, caused severe stress on the Spanish economy and military, resulting in the loss of territory in The Netherlands, and in effect, breaking the back of Spain as a world power. From that time on, Spain simply could not exert the kind of bureaucratic or military control over its colonies that was necessary to prevent eventual revolt. The coup de grâce came in 1808 when Napoleon invaded the Iberian Peninsula, forcing King Ferdinand VII to abdicate in favor of Napoleon's brother. The Portuguese royal family fled to Brazil.

This humiliation delegitimized Spanish imperial control and provided the opportunity for the peripheral elites to exert more local control. In Portugal's case, the fact that the royal family fled to a colony put that colony essentially into a quasi partnership with its imperial master. Not surprisingly, Portuguese Prince Regent Dom João granted Brazil the status of kingdom in 1815.

The fate of Spain was not so clear-cut. A series of liberators emerged—Simón Bolívar, José de San Martín, and Bernardo O'Higgins—and by the late 1820s virtually all of Spain's Latin American colonies had fought their way to independence. The colonies that remained—Cuba, Puerto Rico, and the Philippines—were later lost to the United States in the 1890s. Portugal's colonies in Mozambique, Angola, and Guinea would also fight for their independence, but not until the 1970s.

French and British colonial holdings were lost to the same combination of wars in Europe and independent struggles in the colonies. World War I, while giving them additional territories in the Middle East, actually undermined their capacities in the same way that the Thirty Years' War had undermined Spain's. When this was followed by the Great Depression of the 1930s and then World War II, they were undone, especially with the emergence of the Soviet Union to the east and the United States to the west as the new superpowers, combined with independence movements in the south.

Nationalist unrest in India, fomented by Mahatma Gandhi during the 1920s and 1930s, led to the independence and partition of Pakistan and India in 1947. Israel established its independence inside the Palestinian territory in 1948. By the 1960s, the British had withdrawn from the rest of the Middle East, as well as from Asia and Africa. The French followed suit, particularly after their humiliating defeat at the hands of Ho Chi Minh in Vietnam and Pyrrhic victory in Algeria.

The Soviet empire crumbled under Gorbachev in the late 1980s for reasons having to do most fundamentally with the complete dysfunctionality of a totalitarian system in an increasingly globalizing world, overburdened with military procurements and refusing to allow creativity and freedom for its citizens. Recognizing the limits of a system he could reform but could not change, Gorbachev made the historic decision to peacefully withdraw nine hundred thousand troops from eastern Europe and allow the emergence of independent states throughout the region, leading to the fall of the Berlin Wall in 1989. The machinations of Boris Yeltsin led to the dissolution of the Soviet Union itself in late 1991, leaving only a weakened and turbulent Russia and a series of newly independent and chaotic Euro-Asian republics.

The demise of the European powers, particularly Britain and then the Soviets, has left only the United States as a world power. Behind it lies the long and bloody rise and fall of those empires, which like it, reached for the sky, and as it will, fell to the earth, undone.

7

The Roman Achievement

As the United States embarks on its pathway of supreme power, the crucial question before it is how long it will last before it falls. As a republic, there was nowhere to go but up. As an empire, there is nowhere to go but down. What steps can America take to ensure it remains strong, powerful, and respected by the world over which it now exercises dominion? Is exerting overwhelming military power sufficient, combined with economic exploitation, for America to maintain political control and guarantee wealth to its populace? Or is there some other ingredient that ensures the solidity and coherence of power?

To answer this fundamental question of solidity and coherence, it is illuminating to examine the empire that lasted the longest—Rome—and inquire as to its secrets. Rome's durability was founded not simply on military might or economic gain but on something more fundamental and challenging. Its imperial coherence was ensured by good governance over the empire through institutions that were perceived by the governed as just and fair. This is what Rome achieved and why, of all the empires, it endured the longest and is remembered as the most magnificent.

This is not hyperbole. The great historians, ranging from Gibbon to Durant, assert that the period from 96 A.D. to 180 A.D. constitutes the longest period of continuous good governance in the history of the world. Americans today would like to think that their culture, their democracy, and their political institutions represent the highest reaches of human civilization and governance and that the United States constitutes the vanguard of the human journey. But not so. Even as the ancient Athenians have the accolade for the highest reach of civilization, the ancient Romans have the accolade for the highest reach of continuous good governance. Americans have a long way to go before they join the pantheon of the Athenians and the Romans, whatever their light and whatever their power.

The Romans built the most durable and longest-lasting empire in history because they were quintessentially political in their pursuit of power and legal in their application of mastery. They understood that the victor must rule and that the expression of supremacy must come through law. Because they understood this, they created the greatest system of law in history and an internal coherence that has gone unchallenged by any empire before or since. They taught the world that law is the expression of the consistency of power and that enduring mastery requires the consent of the governed.

The Roman constitution was like that of the British. There was no set document to which everything had to refer. Rather, a stream of precedents provided direction without preventing change. As Rome expanded and conquered, new legislation, issued from assemblies, the senate, and the rulers reached out to the frontiers and brought coherence to the empire. The protection of citizens, the guidance of judges, and the training of lawyers required the organization of jurisprudence into an orderly and accessible form. It was during the second and third centuries A.D. that Roman law was given its final formulation, an achievement comparable to the formulation of science and philosophy by the Greeks.

This Roman accomplishment is of singular importance for the United States to consider as it takes on the challenges of global dominion and optimally, the design of the next phase of global governance. As noted earlier, the forces of democratization, globalization, and communication are transforming the world to such an extent that the prevailing institutions are unable to solve global problems, and the international system of nation-states is in crisis. America has achieved global mastery right at the point when the central question before the international community is how to govern the global system, how to manage it effectively, democratically, and equitably.

As important to the American imperium as military force or economic strength therefore is the question of *governance*. Effective and equitable global governance is the key to American imperial leadership and imperial greatness. In this, the Romans can teach America great lessons, if only Americans have the ears to hear and the humility to listen.

While other states in antiquity developed laws for the governance of states, most notably Hammurabi in Babylonia and Solon in Athens, it was Rome's unique contribution, inspired by Hammurabi, to develop the capacity to unite hundreds of diverse but conquered peoples and thousands of city-states, ranging from Spain in the west to Persia in the east and from England in the north to Egypt in the south, through a unified legal code. Through law, Rome created an imperfect but durable sphere of peace known to both history and legend as *pax Romana*. No other empire achieved such extensive coordination and unification of peoples through the codification of law as did the Romans.

The level of power Rome exercised over most of what was then the known world led to much corruption and many abuses, personified in popular history by the excesses of Nero and Caligula and other lesser-known Caesars. But there were five Caesars, who ruled from 96 to 180 A.D., who understood that for Rome to endure, they had to blend "local" politics with "global" politics and who were compelled by both Roman ideals and personal ethics to use their imperial power for the common good. They did so with a skill and wisdom that gave sublime definition to both imperial power and imperial longevity.

As Gibbon wrote, "If a man were called upon to fix the period in the history of the world during which the condition of the human race was most happy and prosperous, he would without hesitation name that which elapsed from the accession of Nerva to the death of Aurelius. Their united reigns are possibly the only period of history in which the happiness of a great people was the sole object of government."[1]

NERVA   Described as the "reign of the philosopher kings" by William Durant in his masterpiece *The Story of Civilization,* this period began with the Roman senate's appointment of one of its own members, Marcus Cocceuuis Nerva, to replace Emperor Domitian after his assassination in 96 A.D. In so doing, the senate reasserted its right to appoint the king, something it had done during the days of the Roman republic but had forfeited since Julius Caesar had overthrown the republic and usurped absolute power in 45 B.C.

Nerva immediately recalled those who had been exiled by Domitian, returned their land, and freed the Jews from the tribute the emperor Vespasian had exacted on them. He consulted with the senate on all matters, annulled numerous onerous taxes, and established the *alimenta,* a government fund to encourage and finance parentage among the peasantry to increase the population of Italy.

Nerva then proceeded to astound everyone by insisting that his own personal budget and that of the court be brought into order and run with the same frugality by which he insisted on running the government. This act brought the fierce resistance of his Praetorian Guard, who besieged the palace and killed several of his advisers. He offered his throat to the swords of his attackers but was spared. Humiliated, he wished to abdicate, but the senate refused and insisted instead that he follow the example of Augustus and name a successor capable of governing both empire and guard.

This he did, choosing his ablest general, Marcus Ulpius Traianus, remembered by history as Trajan, thus carrying forward the tradition of adoption rather than inheritance in selecting a successor. By the luck of biology, neither Trajan nor his two successors had sons, so each was free to choose as the next emperor that man who was the most suited for office. While this tradition was honored, it provided Rome, according to Durant, with "the finest succession of good and great sovereigns the world has ever had."[2]

TRAJAN   Trajan, age forty-one, was commanding his army in Germany when he received word that Nerva had named him successor. Born in Spain of an Italian family, he was the first non-Roman
to accede to supreme power. The fact that the Roman aristocracy
did not protest this enthronement of a provincial was a major
event and an omen for the rest of Roman history. Trajan heard the
news with Stoic equanimity and took his time, some eighteen
months, to finish his campaign, before riding at the head of his
troops into Rome. His modesty and openness quickly won the
favor of the populace and the senate, and he embarked on a reign
destined to last nineteen years.

Following Nerva, who reigned less than two years, Trajan set
about rationalizing state expenditures, consulting the senate on all
matters, learning, as Durant puts it, that he "might wield absolute
power if he never used absolute speech."[3] He was so frugal an
administrator that he was able to complete extensive public works
without raising taxes. In fact, he lowered taxes, becoming the first
ruler in history to openly publish his annual budget and solicit
scrutiny and criticism.

Trajan thoroughly understood the state budget. He carried on
a meticulous and detailed correspondence with his generals and
governors throughout the empire to ensure that they commanded
and ruled with the same responsibility he exemplified. He honored regions that demonstrated competence and sent envoys to
cities on the point of bankruptcy, particularly in the east, to guide
them back to solvency. Trajan was such a fair and impartial administrator of the laws of Rome that the *Digest* of Justinian ascribes to
him the principle: "It is better that the guilty should remain
unpunished than that the innocent should be condemned."[4]

Trajan was also clearly an imperialist who understood that the
power of Rome was a sacred trust to be extended where possible
and protected at all costs. In the year 101 A.D., within a year of his
accession, he embarked to the Balkans to conquer Dacia, modern-
day Romania, in order to give Rome control of its gold mines and
the trading routes from the Danube to the Black Sea and Asia
Minor. He commanded his armies as he governed Rome: clearly,
decisively, and brilliantly, leading his legions to a swift victory, in
part by bridging the Danube with a structure so innovative that it

was considered one of the engineering marvels of his time. The gold mines of Transylvania were put under imperial control and quickly paid for the expenses of the war.

With the spoils of conquest, Trajan embarked on the greatest program of public works, government aid, and architectural building since Augustus. Like Augustus, he favored Italy over the empire and Rome over Italy. In an effort to spur the economy, he distributed money to any Roman citizen who applied for it, more than three hundred thousand people. His engineers constructed a spacious harbor for Rome, connected to the Tiber River by canals, and finished the public baths begun by Domitian. He repaired the old roads, laid the Via Traiana from Beneventum to Brundisium, built an aqueduct in Ravenna, and erected an amphitheater in Verona. He supplied funding for new roads, buildings, and bridges throughout the length and breadth of the empire. At the same time, he discouraged architectural rivalry between the major cities, urging the governors to spend any surplus on helping the poor. He provided assistance for cities that suffered from fire or the ravages of nature.

More broadly, Trajan promoted agricultural development in Italy by insisting that the aristocracy invest at least a third of their capital in the land. When he saw that this policy was leading to imbalances, he provided state funds for small landowners to purchase and improve their lands. He also extended state mortgage loans at very low interest to Italian peasants and expanded the *alimenta* that Nerva had established to encourage population growth. He established local charity boards to distribute money to poor parents sufficient to provide for the care of their children and was the first emperor to give an allotment of corn to the children of Rome separate from that given to their parents. This care for the poor and children was later expanded by Trajan's successors, Hadrian and Antonius Pius, to other parts of the empire and supplemented by private philanthropy.

His building complete, Trajan decided to take up the task that Julius Caesar had started: to extend and fortify the frontier of the east, securing the trade routes across Armenia and Parthia to central Asia and the Persian Gulf. In 113, he set off with his legions and within a year had subdued Armenia. Over the next four years, he marched through Mesopotamia, overcoming the entire region, conquering even Parthia. He created the provinces of Parthia, Armenia, Assyria, and Mesopotamia and reached the Indian Ocean, the first and last Roman emperor to stand on the shores of that sea. He wrote back to the senate that he had conquered all the lands gained by Alexander the Great but mourned that he was unable to go even farther and conquer the Indus region. He contented himself with building a Red Sea fleet to control commerce with India, left garrisons at all strategic points in the conquered lands, and then reluctantly began his return to Rome.

As Trajan was returning, he was stricken with dropsy and suffered a paralytic stroke. He turned to his nephew Hadrian, gave him command of the main Roman army in Syria, and then had himself carried to the Sicilian coast, hoping to return to Rome, where the senate was preparing the greatest triumph since Augustus. He died at Selinus in 117, at age sixty-four. His ashes were taken back to the capital and buried under a great column that he had erected to be his tomb.

HADRIAN   Historians still debate whether Hadrian, whom Durant describes as "the most brilliant of the Roman emperors,"[5] won the throne because of Trajan's great faith in him or because of his amorous relationship with Trajan's widow. It was probably a combination of both. In any event, he settled the matter by immediately distributing generous amounts of money among the troops, winning their support even if he did not stop their gossip. Like Trajan, he was forty-one upon his accession and considered by friend and foe alike to be the most capable man in the empire.

Hadrian may have been the first Renaissance man. In addition to being a great general and emperor, he read the Stoic philosopher Epictetus extensively and loved to gather scholars and thinkers around him to debate the philosophical issues of the day. He was also a man of the hunt and loved his dogs and horses with such abandon that he had tombs built for his favorites when they died. He was also an accomplished artist, singer, dancer, musician, painter, and author, capable of writing everything from poetry to texts on grammar in both Latin and Greek. He often visited the sick, extended charities to orphans and widows, and was a generous patron to artists, writers, and philosophers.

Hadrian may have also been the first ruler to create a cross-sectoral council of advisers. He chose business executives with experience and ability to administer the government and brought them together with selected senators, aristocrats, jurists, and members of the government to form a *concilium* that met with him on a regular basis to discuss imperial policies.

Hadrian's first act was to revise radically the imperialistic policies of his uncle. He had counseled Trajan against so ambitious a campaign in the east, warning that the lands conquered were too extensive and the demands to keep them subdued too difficult. Preferring to mimic Augustus rather than Alexander, he withdrew the Roman legions from Armenia, Assyria, Mesopotamia, and Parthia. He made Armenia a client kingdom instead of a province and declared the River Euphrates as the eastern boundary of the Roman Empire. He believed it was better to have a smaller, more peaceful empire than one that was extended and turbulent.

Inside secure boundaries, Hadrian focused his considerable talents on governing the empire. He instituted an *advocatus fisci*, an attorney for the treasury, to ensure that everyone who owed taxes paid them as well as to detect corruption and mismanagement. Not surprisingly, although taxes remained the same, revenues increased dramatically. He also oversaw each of his departments of state with such a knowledge of fact and attentiveness to detail that he left his subjects in awe. A Roman historian of the time, Spartianus, observed that "his memory was vast. He wrote, dictated, listened, and conversed with his friends, all at the same time." According to Durant, "Under his care and with the help of an extended civil service, the empire was probably better governed than ever before or afterward."[6]

Hadrian understood that a unified legal code would keep the empire intact and operating smoothly. He worked tirelessly to bring order to the rather chaotic accumulation of laws, imperial edicts, and juridical traditions that he had inherited and through which the empire was rather haphazardly governed. He convened a body of jurists as part of his privy council and commissioned them to replace the annual edicts of the praetors with a "perpetual edict" to be observed by all future judges in Italy. One of his jurists, Salvius Julianus, a Roman of African birth, demonstrated such genius as legal adviser to the emperor that the senate voted him double the usual salary. It was he who formulated the perpetual edict and the systematic codification of civil and praetorian law for which Rome is so famous.

With Salvius Julianus at his side, Hadrian acted as a supreme arbiter both in Rome and on his journeys and earned the reputation as a fair and wise judge, stern but merciful. His decrees generally favored the weaker over the stronger, the slave over the master, the poor over the rich, the small landowner over the big landowner, and the consumer over merchants and traders. Durant describes him "not as a radical reformer; he was only a superlative administrator seeking, within the limits and inequalities of human nature, the greatest good of the whole. He preserved old forms, but he quietly poured new content into them according to the needs of the time."[7]

Hadrian probably took a greater interest in the empire as a whole than any Roman emperor before or after him. Following the example of Augustus, he decided to visit every province in the empire. He left Rome in 121 surrounded not simply by courtiers, harem, and guard but also by engineers, interpreters, scholars, architects, and artists. He journeyed first to Germany, where he closely scrutinized the military defenses against the empire's future invaders. He issued severe regulations to ensure military discipline and made an example of himself, obeying all his own rules. He ate and slept with his men and never used a chariot, walking with full equipment twenty miles a day, surpassing all those around him in endurance and equanimity in the face of exhaustion, heat, and thirst. He issued orders to increase the pay and the quality of weapons for all his legions, even relaxing their discipline during off-hours providing they kept themselves vigilant and battle-ready. The Roman army was never better trained than during Hadrian's reign, Rome's boundaries never more secure, its enemies never more subdued.

For five years Hadrian traveled his empire, reaching England from Germany, where he built a wall against the barbarians. He then traveled to Gaul, Spain, and northwest Africa, where he subdued the Moors, and then eastward, visiting Asia Minor, building in Nicomedia a temple that was considered one of the seven wonders of the ancient world. In Athens, he saw architectural decay and extensive unemployment and embarked on a building program so ambitious that when it was completed, Athens was cleaner, more prosperous, and more beautiful than it had been even during its golden age under Pericles.

Traveling down through Palestine, he saw that Jerusalem was still in ruins from the siege and sack of the city by the emperor Titus some sixty years earlier. He ordered the city rebuilt and renamed Aelia Capitolina. He then went on to Alexandria, where he expanded the museum, renovated Pompey's tomb, and took a leisurely sail up the Nile. On his way back to Rome, he stopped in Sicily to climb eleven thousand feet to the top of Mount Etna to witness the sunrise.

Finally back in Rome in 131, Hadrian realized that he had one last task to complete: to make Rome more beautiful than ever before. The entire city was examined and more than one hundred buildings erected, restored, or repaired. Modestly, he inscribed his name on none of them. His most famous reconstruction was of the Pantheon, which had the largest dome in history and became the model for St. Peter's Basilica and the Capitol in Washington, D.C.

As his life drew to a close, Hadrian could feel that he had made the empire better than he had found it. Never before, not even under Augustus, had it been so prosperous or ruled so benevolently. Augustus had thought of the provinces as lucrative appendages to Italy, to be husbanded for Italy's sake, even as Italy was husbanded for the sake of Rome. Under Hadrian, Rome became not a tax collector to Italy and the empire but the responsible administrator of an empire in which all parts alike received the care of the government. Under his rule, the empire became a realm in which the Greek sprit ruled the east and the mind as openly as the Roman spirit ruled the state and the west. Hadrian had seen it all and had made it one. As Durant describes it,

Hadrian had promised that he "would manage the commonwealth as conscious that it was the people's property, not his own, and he had kept his promise. . . . No other man ever built so plentifully, no other ruled so directly."[8]

The only turbulence suffered during his waning years was the revolt of the Jews in 135, which he expeditiously crushed. In that same year, age fifty-nine, he suffered a painful illness similar to tuberculosis and dropsy, which slowly wasted his body and crushed his spirit. Knowing he was about to die, he designated his close friend Lucius Verus (the elder) as his successor, only to see him die within months. So he turned to another friend, Titus Aurelius Antonius, and adopted him as his successor, asking him in turn to adopt as his sons two young men, one of whom was the future Marcus Aurelius, in order to begin their training for eventual rule.

Hadrian's sickness and suffering increased. Blood often gushed from his nostrils. He longed for death and ordered his servants and doctors to put him out of his misery, only to be refused. He openly mourned that he, who had the power of life and death over an entire empire, was unable to order his own death. So he withdrew to his villa outside Rome and fed himself on food and drink that he thought would hasten his end. He finally succumbed in 138, in the twenty-first year of his reign, leaving behind a short poem for his subjects to ponder:

> Soul of mine, pretty one, flitting one,
> Guest and partner of my clay,
> Whither wilt thou hide away—
> Pallid one, rigid one, naked one,
> Never to play again, never to play?[9]

ANTONIUS PIUS   Antonius ascended the throne at the age of fifty-one, one of the wealthiest men in Rome. His first act was to pour his personal fortune into the imperial treasury. He then canceled arrears in taxes, distributed money to the citizens, paid for numerous games and contests, and ensured that the staples of wheat, oil, and wine were in bountiful supply and distributed free. He moderated Hadrian's stern reprisals against the Jews and extended his lenience toward the Christians. He continued Hadrian's building programs throughout the empire and managed the state finances so effectively that by the time of his death the treasury had the largest surplus in Rome's history. He was unique among emperors in providing receipts and records of his personal expenditures for public record.

Antonius followed Hadrian's reform and codification of the law by bringing to Roman jurisprudence the influence of Stoic philosophy. In this, Antonius permitted a profound Greek influence to crown Rome's greatest achievement. The Stoics declared that law should accord with morality and that innocence or guilt should be determined by the intention of the actor, not the results of the action. They taught two supreme principles that became the basis of all subsequent civilized jurisprudence: cases in doubt should be adjudicated in favor of the accused, and everyone should be considered innocent until proven guilty.

Antonius made the penalties for adultery the same for both men and women and did more to make the treatment of slaves humane than had any of his predecessors. He passed laws that penalized owners who mistreated slaves, restricted the torture of slaves at trials, and pronounced severe punishment for any owner who killed a slave. He was also one of the first emperors to value education for more than just the aristocracy. He encouraged education with state funds, initiated educational programs for children of the poor, and bestowed on teachers some of the privileges accorded to the senatorial class.

Antonius so loved Rome that he never left it, choosing to govern his vast empire through deputies whom he trusted to be competent and honest. He had to wage a few wars to quell rebellions in Dacia, Achaea, and Egypt but followed Hadrian's wisdom in fortifying cautious frontiers and ensuring that his legions were well managed and supplied. Intending to keep the empire safe without war, he often quoted the saying of the philosopher Scipio: "It is better to save a single citizen than to slay a thousand foes." The empire was safe and well governed under him; indeed, it was during his reign that the term *pax Romana* was coined by the leading commentators of the day, who included the Stoic Epictetus, the writer Philo, and the historian Plutarch. "Never had monarchy left men so free, or so respected the rights of its subjects," says Durant. "The world's ideal seemed to have been attained. Wisdom reigned, and for twenty-three years the world was governed by a father."[10]

It only remained for Antonius to crown a good life with a peaceful death, something this astonishing man proceeded to do. In the year 161, at the ripe old age of seventy-four, he was seized by a high fever and stomach disorder. He called Marcus Aurelius to his bedside and calmly committed to him the affairs of the state, instructing his servants to transfer the golden statue of Fortuna, the goddess of fortune, from his bedchamber to that of Marcus. He then fell peacefully asleep and did not wake again.

Of Antonius, says Durant, "There is no history, for he had almost no faults and committed no crimes . . . he gave the Empire the most equitable, and not the least efficient, government it would ever have."[11] At his funeral, the senate bestowed on him the accolade *Pius* because he embodied the Roman virtues and personified the *Optimus Princeps,* the best of princes.

MARCUS AURELIUS   Marcus Aurelius, remembered by history as the author of *Meditations,* grew up during the reign of Antonius Pius, knowing that he would succeed him. He was perhaps the best educated of any of the Roman emperors, enjoying the benefit of seventeen academic tutors, being immersed in the ritual and mysteries of the temple and cult, and being trained as a soldier and hunter. At the age of twelve, he took on the rough cloak of philosopher and insisted on sleeping on the floor instead of in a bed, resisting the entreaties of his mother for the comforts of wealth. As Durant describes it, "He became a Stoic before he became a man."[12]

In his *Meditations,* written much later, he bade himself, "Do everything as a disciple of Antonius, remember his constancy in every reasonable act, his evenness in all things, his piety, and the serenity of his countenance, and his disregard of empty fame . . . with how little he was satisfied; how laborious and patient, how religious without superstition."[13]

When he succeeded Antonius in 161, all of Rome and the empire proclaimed him as the embodiment of Plato's ideal philosopher king. Marcus himself was much more modest: "Never hope to realize Plato's Republic," he wrote. "Let it be sufficient that you have in some degree ameliorated mankind, and do not think such improvement a matter of small importance. Who can change the opinions of men? And without a change of sentiments what can you make but reluctant slaves and hypocrites?"[14]

But there were difficulties ahead. Despite his philosophical orientation, or perhaps because of it, Marcus Aurelius made several crucial mistakes that were to bring to a close the lengthy era of good governance that began with Nerva. His first error was to designate Lucius Verus (the younger, son of Lucius Verus, Sr., who had been named by Hadrian as successor, only to die), who had also been adopted by Antonius Pius as a son, as full colleague and co-emperor, even though he was completely unsuited for the task and would cause Aurelius numerous disappointments and failures. More seriously, this established the precedent of joint rule, which would later weaken and eventually help to break up the empire.

Second, Marcus was too generous with public funds, spending money he could not afford to spend and giving the populace a false sense of security at a time when the frontiers were being attacked. Discipline, not indulgence, would have better served the empire.

Finally, Marcus appointed his biological son, Commodus, as his heir, even though he was as cruel, corrupt, and inept as any of the worst emperors to sit upon the Roman throne. He thus ended the successor selection process that had given him the throne and had ensured such a lengthy span of good governance.

Still, Marcus was a wise ruler. He continued the legal reforms of Hadrian, gave the *alimenta* its widest expression, and after the death of his wife, created an endowment for the aid of young women. He also did everything he could to moderate the gladiator contests in the arenas. However, the philosopher king was destined not to reign in peace but to be challenged by war. In 162, revolt broke out in Britain, the Chatti invaded Germany, and the Parthian king declared war on Rome. Marcus dispatched his best generals to deal with these challenges but made another crucial mistake by sending Lucius Verus to take on the Parthians.

Lucius got no further than Antioch, where he fell in love with a beautiful courtesan and stayed in the city to cavort, allowing the Parthians to run amok throughout Syria and the east. Marcus did not chide Lucius but only ordered the general second in command to force the Parthians back and secure the borders once again in Mesopotamia. Lucius did return to Rome for the triumph but unknowingly brought back an insidious plague with his troops.

The plague rapidly swept through Asia Minor, Egypt, Greece, Gaul, and Italy, and within one year (166–167) killed more people than had been lost in all the various wars Marcus had waged. In Rome, two thousand people died in a single day. Marcus did everything he could to mitigate this scourge, but knowing nothing about contagion or hygiene, could only watch helplessly as people died and the plague spread.

In the midst of this tragedy, news came that the barbarians of the north had crossed the Danube, overcome a Roman garrison of twenty-thousand soldiers, and were pouring down into the Balkans, over the Alps, and even threatening Venice. Not since Hannibal nearly three centuries before had Rome been so threatened, and Marcus reacted commensurately. He immediately drafted every able-bodied man he could find into an army that had been depleted by plague, enrolling everyone from gladiators, policemen, slaves, and mercenaries. He raised funds for the campaign by auctioning off the crown jewels, objects of art, and clothing from the imperial palaces in the Forum. He then led his legions to attack the barbarians, forcing them completely out of Roman territory and back across the Danube.

The victory gave him only a brief respite. In 169–170, the Chatti invaded again across the Rhine; the Costoboii crossed the Balkans into Greece, getting to within fourteen miles of Athens; and a new tribe, the Lombards, appeared in Germany. Marcus understood that it was now war to the death, and he mobilized his assets and legions accordingly. Thus began the Second Marcomannic War, which lasted from 169 to 175, during which time Marcus routed the barbarians once again, forcing them back as far as Bohemia. Always the philosopher, it was during this time that, fighting by day, he wrote his famous *Meditations* by night. But at the height of his success, he was informed by his spies that Avidius

Cassius, a general he had dispatched to Egypt to quell a rebellion there, had declared himself emperor and was marching on Rome.

Marcus quickly negotiated a peace settlement with the barbarian tribes, annexing a ten-mile strip of land north of the Danube and leaving a string of fortified garrisons on the southern side. He marched with his main legions toward Asia Minor, only to learn that Cassius had been killed by a loyal centurion. Nevertheless, Marcus continued his march, reaching Alexandria, where he rested, replacing his armor with a philosopher's mantle. He walked the city without a guard, attended lectures of the leading teachers of the region, and enjoyed discourse with the intellectuals and sages.

In the fall of 176, after almost seven years of war, Marcus returned to Rome and was given a triumphal celebration as savior of the empire. At his side rode Commodus, a boy of fifteen, whom he designated as his colleague on the throne. The plague had burned itself out by then and the city was returning to normalcy. As Durant describes it, "The capital had suffered little from the wars, which had been financed with remarkable economy and little extra taxation; while the battle raged on the frontiers trade flourished within, and money jingled everywhere. It was the height of Rome's tide and of its Emperor's popularity; all the world acclaimed him as at once a soldier, a sage, and a saint."[15]

But Marcus knew that the barbarians were only temporarily weakened, and that despite a hundred defeats they were in fact growing stronger. He believed that further invasions would cease only if Rome extended its boundaries to the mountains of Bohemia, so in 178 he set off with Commodus and his legions for the Third Marcomannic War. Again he crossed the Danube and wiped out any resistance and was about to proclaim Bohemia and Danubian Galicia new provinces when death struck. He called Commodus to his side and bade him finish the task and realize the dream of Augustus to extend the borders of Rome to the Elbe. He then refused all further food and drink for the next six days. On the seventh, he rose from his bed and presented Commodus as the new emperor. He then returned to bed, covered his head with a sheet, and died.

Commodus did not follow his father's admonition. Rather, he quickly made peace with the barbarians and returned to Rome, where he preoccupied himself with participating in gladiatorial contests and debauchery. He drank and gambled, kept a harem of three hundred women and three hundred boys, paraded himself as a transvestite at public games, and enjoyed the spectacle of unspeakable cruelties perpetrated by gladiators on the defenseless. He consigned the governance of the empire to a series of incompetent and rapacious friends, until finally, in the year 192, he was poisoned by one of them and then strangled while he lay in the bath. He was thirty-one.

The time of the philosopher kings was over. As Gibbon marks it, the decline of Rome had begun. When Marcus reigned, says Durant,

> Rome had reached the apex of her curve and was already touched with decay. Her boundaries had been extended beyond the Danube into Scotland and the Sahara, into the Caucasus and Russia, and to the gates of Parthia. She had accomplished for that confusion of peoples and faiths, a unity not of language and culture, but at least of economy and law. She had woven it into a majestic commonwealth, within which the exchange of goods moved in unprecedented plenty and freedom; and for two centuries she had guarded the great realm from barbarian inroads and had given it security and peace. All the white man's world looked to her as the center of the universe, the omnipotent and eternal city. Never had there been such wealth, such splendor, or such power.[16]

Nevertheless, in the midst of all the prosperity and splendor of the second century, the seeds of decay that would ruin Rome in the third century took root. Marcus contributed to the decay by naming Commodus as his successor and by fighting wars that centralized ever more authority into the hands of the emperor. Commodus simply kept in peace those prerogatives his father had gained by war. As in other empires, local and private initiative withered as power was centralized in the state, and wealth was drained away as the ever-growing bureaucracy and endless campaigns to shore up the frontiers demanded more and more taxation to raise more and more money.

Massive government expenditures for war and indiscriminate handouts to the populace eventually exhausted the treasury and debased the currency. Because the emperor had almost all the power, the citizens lost any sense of civic virtue and insisted the government take responsibility. Cynicism replaced patriotism, and indolence superceded sacrifice. The wealthy withdrew more and more from public life, scheming new ways to avoid taxes and keep their sons from military service.

In the meantime, the provinces were recovering from their conquest and flourishing in the *pax Romana* in which they were included, successfully competing with Italy. The provinces began to replenish the Roman legions, and soon their armies held Italy at their mercy. Their generals became Rome's emperors. The empire was built with Italy conquering the world. After Marcus, that empire would conquer the conquerors. All the while, the barbarians outside the empire probed and exploited any weakness, taking land, forcing concessions, and by the fifth century, finally overcoming most of the western empire and sacking Rome itself.

THE GREATNESS THAT WAS ROME   Even in falling from greatness, Rome was noble. So strong was its social cohesion, so powerful its legions, so durable its government that it took as long to unravel as to build. As Durant observes:

> The Roman state committed a thousand political crimes; it built its edifice upon a selfish oligarchy and an obscurantist priesthood; it achieved a democracy of freemen, and then destroyed it with corruption and violence; it exploited its conquests to support a parasitic Italy, which, when it could no longer exploit, it collapsed. . . . But amid all this evil it formed a majestic system of law which through nearly all Europe gave security to life and property, and incentive and continuity to industry.[17]

Rome conquered the Mediterranean world and adopted its culture, giving it order, prosperity, and peace for over two centuries, holding back the barbarians for two centuries more, and even in collapse, transmitting the classic heritage of antiquity to the West. Put simply, says Durant, "Rome has had no rival in the art of government."[18]

Rome developed a government of checks and balances between the legislative and executive branches that inspired the revolutionaries of eighteenth-century France and America. For a time, monarchy, aristocracy, and democracy were enmeshed so successfully that Rome governed with justice and gained the loyalty of an entire empire. It built municipal institutions and extended municipal freedoms to cities throughout the empire. In essence, Rome built a culture that was Greek in spirit, but Roman in application. Rome was too engrossed in military conquest and governance to develop the lofty idealism or philosophy of the Greeks, but it appreciated Greek democracy and wisdom, absorbed them, along with the wise traditions of Egypt and Carthage, and reworked them in a manner that both inspired and aided in the governing of the realm.

Rome did not invent education but developed it to a scale unknown in the ancient world, giving it state support, providing it to girls as well as boys, and the poor as well as the rich. It developed a curriculum that has been used in Europe until the present day. Rome did not invent the arch, the vault, or the dome, but Romans used them with such brilliance that in some fields of architecture, their achievements are still unequaled. From the medieval cathedrals to the Capitol in Washington, D.C., modern structures were made in Rome's memory and style. Rome's Latin tongue was brilliantly corrupted to form the basis of French, Italian, Spanish, Portuguese, and even much of English. Latin was the *lingua franca* in Europe until the eighteenth century, and survives even today in the sonorous ritual and official documents of the Roman Catholic Church.

Rome made few advancements in science and few mechanical improvements in industry, but the Romans enriched the world by allowing commerce over secure seas and reliable roads. Along Roman trading routes and over a thousand Roman bridges, there passed to the medieval and modern worlds the ancient techniques of art, tillage, handicraft, monument building, military hospitals, sanitation, investment and banking, and innumerable varieties of fruits and plants, almost all of which were brought from the East to be reworked and take root in the West.

Rome provided the elixir of ideas, practicality, governance, and commerce that defined imperial greatness. Says Durant: "It administered its empire at first with greed and cruelty, then with such tolerance and essential justice that the great realm has never again known a like content. It made the desert blossom with civilization, and atoned for its sins with the miracle of a lasting peace. Today our highest labors seek to revive the *pax Romana* for a disordered world."[19]

8

America at the Choice Point

IT IS AGAINST THE BACKGROUND of the history of empire and the greatness of Rome that it must be noted that the decisions being made by the Bush administration are almost all with specific reference to a very finite event: the trauma of September 11, 2001. Both the attack and the subsequent war on terrorism characterize the present American moment and predominant focus of the U.S. government. Historical legacies and global complexities are being viewed through the very narrow lens provided by a single experience.

Is there any way that this occasion can be a gateway to the larger issues? This is a difficult task because the wounds of September 11 continue to be quite raw, particularly in the American psyche. The initial American response, still with us, has been bewilderment and hurt that anyone would want to do such a thing to the United States. These notions were combined with the demand for vengeance. The U.S. government marched onto the world stage, overthrew the Taliban in Afghanistan with international support, and then invaded Iraq without it. Few acknowledged that the nation was in the grip of a Jacksonian act of vengeance or that it might be affected by a form of post-traumatic stress disorder.

In the discussion of 9/11 in chapter 1, the point was made that in the aftermath of trauma there is often a bifurcation in the affected group between community and lawlessness. This means that there is always a choice between compassion and aggression when one responds to a hurt. How the U.S. government reacted was the result of specific choices made by President Bush and his administration, which in turn had a major effect on how the American people interpreted and responded to the experience.

Mary Robinson, then U.N. High Commissioner for Human Rights and now the director of the Ethical Globalization Initiative, suggested immediately after the attack that it should have been defined not as an act of terrorism but as a crime against humanity. Defining the attack as terrorism and then declaring a war on terrorism, she maintained, did two things: it gave mere criminals the status of soldiers, and it set the entire aftermath of 9/11 within the context of conflict.

Defining the events as crimes against humanity would have relegated Osama bin Laden and al-Qaeda to the status of common criminals and mass murderers, and it would have generated a human rights and humanitarian context for both American and international reactions. This would have enabled the Americans certainly to conduct military reprisals but it would have also allowed for a more comprehensive exploration of some of the underlying social and human rights issues involved.

The war on terrorism was a choice, it was not an inevitability. President Bush chose war. He divided the world starkly into good and evil, vowing to lead the forces of light to triumph over the forces of darkness. There was great power in this simple vision, because the light motif is so deeply embedded in American history and self-perception and because the need for revenge was so strongly felt.

Not for an instant did the president or even most Americans consider the possibility that the attack had something to do with how the United States was comporting itself in the world. To the contrary. "They hate our freedoms," Bush said repeatedly. Like generations of Americans before him, he fused America's self-interest with America's ideals. To attack the one was to attack the other. To damage American commercial assets was to violate American liberty. This logic led to the war on terrorism and the administration's demand that the entire world take sides.

Because the president saw it as a referendum on American primacy, he challenged nations either to support the war on terrorism or risk sharing the same fate as the terrorists. This referendum took place over the crisis with Iraq. What the United States saw was that, if forced to choose, most of the world stood against America, or at least chose to abstain from overt collaboration with it.

In defining the American response to 9/11 as a war, the Bush administration was able to use the occasion to refine American foreign policy and enunciate the Bush doctrine: henceforth, the United States will engage in "anticipatory self-defense" and "pre-emptive deterrence" in order to combat the evils of terrorism. It will use any force necessary to ensure that no other power even attempts to challenge its military dominance. In this sense, 9/11 provided both a cause and an opportunity. It was the cause of the war on terrorism and it was the opportunity to expand American military power massively around the world. As Secretary of State Colin Powell stated, "Not only is the Cold War over, the post–Cold War period is also over."[1]

In this new era, President Bush stated, "America will lead the world to peace." Under his watch, he asserts, the U.S. government intends to persevere in its historic mission to shape the international order in line with both American ideals and American interests. In the view of the president, America will seek a free but orderly world, employing for that purpose the military and economic power America has aggregated over the past two centuries of imperial climb. The president has made it clear to the world that the United States has no intention of relinquishing the power it has gained.

Although these choices, policies, and actions may be natural responses for a nation that suffered such an enormous blow so soon after reaching global preeminence, they are based on an extremely simplified worldview. The reality that gave rise to 9/11 is far more multifaceted. Great events, particularly when viewed from a distance, are invariably composed of light and dark dimensions that combine into subtle hues that change over time. Mary Robinson was getting at some of the deeper issues, and there are other aspects to explore as well.

Before exploring them, however, it must be said that any wisdom gained in trying to understand momentous events, particularly those in which one is actually involved, is often elusive. As T. S. Eliot said, people often "have the experience but miss the meaning." Invariably, understanding comes slowly, painfully, and only after deep reflection. In other words, our thoughts change as our subjective interactions with the event deepens, as they will in this case with the passage of time and America's own maturation in the ebb and flow of world events. In ten years, and certainly in a hundred years, America and the world will look back on September 11 and view it completely differently than those of us who lived through the events do today.

What we can say with reasonable confidence now is that the Jacksonian response of the U.S. government to the tragedy of 9/11 has temporarily cut America off from the world. This chapter will explore other ways of interpreting the event, in the hopes that America can be opened to the world again and find the gateway to the kind of global leadership the world needs it to exercise.

UNDERSTANDING THE ROOTS OF TERRORISM   Ironically, while 9/11 is considered an American tragedy, nearly as many non-Americans as Americans died when the Twin Towers came crashing down. The World Trade Center exemplified globalization as few buildings did, with people from literally all over the world coming together there to further global commerce. In an act watched live by millions of people worldwide, the international community was given the opportunity to mourn its dead and to reflect on humanity's incapacity to be consistently humane.

As painful as it was, what America suffered on 9/11 is what others throughout the world have already experienced, sometimes with even more devastating impact and sometimes at the hands of Americans. In the aftermath of the traumas the United States has caused them, they have felt the same need to hit back as the Americans did after 9/11. From the point of view of their enemies, Americans are guilty of major crimes against them, thus their hatred and violence against the United States. The Indian author Arundhati Roy spoke for many, particularly in the global south, when she wrote immediately after 9/11:

> Who is Osama bin Laden? He is America's family secret. He is the American president's dark doppelganger, the savage twin of all that purports to be beautiful and civilized. He has been sculpted from the spare rib of a world laid to waste by America's foreign policy: its gunboat diplomacy, its nuclear arsenal, its vulgarly stated policy of "full spectrum dominance," its chilling disregard for non-American lives, its barbarous military interventions, its support for despotic and dictatorial regimes, its merciless economic agenda that has munched through the economies of poor countries like a cloud of locusts, and its marauding multinationals who are taking over the air we breathe, the ground we stand on, the water we drink, the thoughts we think.[2]

Osama bin Laden did to the United States what many around the world wanted to see happen. For many, the attacks of 9/11 meant that America was finally getting its due. In its more than two centuries of imperial climb, the United States has gained much power but has also made many enemies. Every time it has won, someone else has lost. Especially during the Cold War, when the United States supported authoritarian and corrupt military regimes throughout the global south while U.S. corporations ruthlessly pursued markets and economic advantage, America created a pervasive antipathy against its power.

In the Middle East in particular, the one-sided support of the United States for the state of Israel against the Arabs and the Palestinians generated ever-deepening hostility. Israel was established, expanded, and protected with massive and continuous American aid. The pervasive resentment of Arabs for the United States is deeply embedded in their resistance to Israel.

Osama bin Laden and his followers, therefore, are not an isolated cult like the Branch Davidians or alienated loners like Timothy McVeigh or the Unabomber. They come out of a whole culture that reinforces their hostility and distrust of the West generally and of America in particular. To say that al-Qaeda is an isolated network may be reassuring, but it is false.

Palestinians danced in the streets of the West Bank when they heard the news of 9/11. The Arab press was replete with nuanced but unambiguous expressions of admiration for bin Laden. For them, September 11 was not mindless terrorism for terrorism's sake. It was retribution and revenge.

The reality is that Osama bin Laden is acting with the support of millions of people across the Islamic world and throughout the global south. He has become almost a Robin Hood-like figure, hitting out against the bad Sheriff of Nottingham and then disappearing into Sherwood Forest, only to reappear again when least expected. It is because of their widespread support that bin Laden and most of his leadership were able to melt back into the communities out of which they originally came and elude American capture. It is also the reason why, even after the collapse of the Taliban in Afghanistan and the invasion of Iraq, al-Qaeda was able to launch coordinated assaults on symbols of American power throughout the Middle East. Even many of those working with the Americans in their war on terrorism are secretly supporting bin Laden, something especially true in Saudi Arabia. Hatred against America is not something bin Laden generated. It is something produced by America itself through its protection of Israel and the consolidation of its own imperial power in the region, with bases in Saudi Arabia, Afghanistan, Kuwait, Qatar, and now Iraq.

Isolated madmen bent on random destruction do not plan acts like those of September 11, which needed a high degree of sophistication and precision. Those acts were deliberatively conceived, meticulously planned, and methodically executed by people of such deep conviction that they were willing to give their very lives to achieve the success of their mission.

It is a level of commitment and depth few of us can even imagine. The only modern equivalent is the Japanese kamikaze pilots of World War II, more than four thousand of whom flew to their certain deaths. From October 25, 1944 until the end of the war, they carried out aerial suicide missions against incredulous Americans for whom such acts of self-sacrifice were completely incomprehensible. This marked the first time in history that suicide missions were organized on a sustained and massive scale. What is astonishing is that the Japanese ran out of planes long before they ran out of volunteers. Furthermore, until the very end, they flew their missions with the fervent support of the entire population of Japan.

THE ROLE OF RELIGIOUS FUNDAMENTALISM   What deepens Osama bin Laden's power and appeal is that he is dedicated to more than merely war. From his perspective, he is not engaging in mere terrorism, defined as the wanton destruction of civilians. He is leading a *jihad*, a holy war, against the United States and Israel. In so doing, he is tapping into the deepest roots of Islamic civilization and history. From the very genesis of Islam, the prophet Muhammad divided the world into believers and nonbelievers, an image the psychologist Elias Canetti captures powerfully in his book *Crowds and Power*:

> When the trumpet of the Last Judgment sounds the dead all rise from their graves and rush to the Field of Judgment "like men rallying to a Standard." There they take up their station before God, in two mighty crowds separated from each other, the faithful on one side and the unbelieving on the other; and each individual is judged by God. . . . The bi-partition of the crowd in Islam is unconditional. The faithful and the unbelieving are fated to be separate forever and to fight each other. The war of religion is a sacred duty and thus, though in a less comprehensive form, the double crowd of the Last Judgment is prefigured in every earthly battle.[3]

This image is, of course, very similar to that of the Jewish and Christian apocalyptic traditions. The fundamentalists of all three monotheistic religions hold essentially the same views, albeit with different details and emphases. The world is divided into believers and nonbelievers. God is on "our" side, and in the end, will destroy the infidels.

For millions of evangelical Christian believers across America, for example, the return of the Jews to Palestine and the establishment of the state of Israel in 1948 marked the beginning of the last generation on earth before Jesus comes again and the world is destroyed at the hands of an angry God.

According to a Times/CNN poll released by *Time* magazine in its cover story on the subject in July 2002, 36 percent of all Americans believe that the Bible is the word of God and to be interpreted literally. Fifty-nine percent believe that the prophecies of the Book of Revelation will come true. Seventeen percent believe that the end of the world will take place in their lifetime. Thirty-six percent support Israel because they believe in biblical prophecies that the Jews must control all of Jerusalem, including the Temple Mount, before Jesus will come again.

Books and Web sites abound that interpret current events in the context of expectations that our generation will see the end of the world. *The Late Great Planet Earth* by Hal Lindsay was the biggest-selling book of the 1970s. *The Left Behind* series by Tim LeHaye and Jerry Jenkins was second only to the Harry Potter books as the biggest-sellers of the 1990s. The ninth book in the series, *Desecration*, was the best-selling book of 2001, with 3.1 million copies sold. The tenth book, *The Remnant*, was the biggest selling book of 2002, with an initial print run of 2.75 million in hard cover.

One Web site—raptureready.com—has a "Rapture Index" that tracks indicators that contribute to worldwide instability and turbulence, from earthquakes, floods, plagues, and wars to civil unrest and unemployment. A reading over 154 means that the end could come at any time. The index hit an all-time high on September 24, 2001, when it reached 182.

The theology expressed in the *Left Behind* series and the Rapture Index, which is preached from thousands of pulpits throughout evangelical America, is based on a very specific interpretation of the Bible, especially the Book of Revelation but also including the Gospels and the prophetic books of the Old Testament such as Daniel, Ezekiel, Jeremiah, and Isaiah. The basic belief is that God created the world and will end the world. As already noted, the return of the Jews to Palestine and the establishment of the state of Israel in 1948 were the key indicators that the end is near. These events mark the beginning of the last generation before the apocalyptic destruction of the world. As the final drama of history unfolds, according to this view, the planetary ecology will become increasingly turbulent and human affairs increasingly destructive.

In the midst of this planetary turmoil, Jesus Christ will return from heaven and in a great "rapture," will snatch up all Christians and take them back to heaven with him. Then will begin a seven-year period of "tribulation," during which an Antichrist figure will emerge who promises peace but delivers war. God will pour out the vials of divine wrath all over the world, creating unprecedented environmental dislocation and societal havoc. At the end of the seven years, Jesus will return a second time and establish a thousand-year reign of peace. A new heaven and a new earth will be created for believers. Satan and his angels, along with the disbelievers, will be thrown into a bottomless pit where they will burn in fire and brimstone forever.

The political ideology fostered by this apocalyptic theology combines a radical pessimism about human nature and current events with an equally radical optimism about God's plan for the elect. Quite literally, the worse the world situation becomes, the more expectant these believers become because they believe they are getting closer to Jesus's coming again and taking them to heaven. They have little regard for the environment because they believe the environment will be destroyed anyway. They have little sympathy for the poor and the dispossessed because they believe that economic dislocation and civil unrest are indicators of human depravity and a signal that the end is nigh. They have little support for the protection of civil liberties because they believe that strong action must be taken against the infidels and potential terrorists.

A central part of the politics of evangelical apocalyptic belief is radical support for Israel. In the Times/CNN poll, 42 percent of all Americans support Israel because they believe that the Jews are God's chosen people. They believe that Israel is destined to take over all the land of "Greater Israel," which extends into Syria and includes all of the West Bank. They believe that Israel will some day soon build a replica of Solomon's temple on the Dome of the Rock, where the al-Aqsa Mosque—considered holy by the Muslims—currently stands.

American Christian evangelical politics is also characterized by a deep suspicion and mistrust of the United Nations. In the *Left Behind* books, the Antichrist is a Russian diplomat who is elected as secretary-general of the United Nations. He is depicted as the epitome of cunning, manipulation, and evil. The establishment of the European Union, in particular the adoption of the euro as the single currency of Europe, is taken as one of the signs of the end.

Evangelical theology and its political agenda are particularly significant because President Bush himself is a born-again Christian with deep sympathy for the evangelical tradition. Several of his cabinet members are similarly oriented, especially Donald Evans, the secretary of commerce, who was instrumental in Bush's actual conversion to evangelical Christianity and remains one of his closest friends and advisers.

Religious fundamentalism has always played an important role in American politics. From the Puritans in colonial America, to the abolitionists and the missionaries of the 1800s, and the Moral Majority and the Christian Coalition of the 1980s, religion has been a potent political instrument in American domestic and foreign affairs. During the Reagan administration, the president, Secretary of Defense Casper Weinberger, and Secretary of the Interior James Watt all spoke publicly of their resonance with evangelical Christianity and apocalyptic theology. Reagan's famous "evil empire" speech about the Soviet Union was made before the National Association of Evangelicals.

The degree of influence and power of the Christian right on specific policy formations and actions of the Bush administration is difficult to determine. But the fact that there *is* a potent evangelical Christian political constituency with dark visions of apocalyptic belief is very important to note. Both Americans and the larger world community should be aware of it, because it is unquestionably contributing to the Bush administration's policies in the Middle East.

The power of religious fundamentalism in the United States is mirrored in the Middle East. In Israel, religious fundamentalists have a lock on the conservative Likud Party and have actively participated in most of the governing coalitions, whether led by Likud or the more liberal Labor Party. They dominate the social, political, and security debate with the same dogmatic clarity as the fundamentalists in Washington. They believe that the Jews have a divine right to the entire territory controlled by King David in ancient Israel, that Israel's national security is paramount and can only be maintained by overwhelming force, and that God is on the side of Israel as much now as in antiquity. Even more powerful than they are in the United States, religious fundamentalists in Israel have succeeded in forcing through laws that have ensured that Israel became and remains a religious as opposed to a secular state.

In turn, Islamic fundamentalism has its own version of dogmatic certainty, mostly around the strict application of *sharia* law in everyday life and the subordination and seclusion of women. What is uniquely powerful in Islam is the concept of holy war as a virtue. Holy war is elevated to a sacred calling, often placed along with the five "pillars of Islam" established by Muhammad: praying five times a day toward Mecca, giving alms to the poor, making the pilgrimage to Mecca, keeping the fast of Ramadan, and making the Islamic declaration of faith, "There is no God but God and Muhammad is his prophet."

In fact, if we take a look back at the history of Islam, we can trace the spiritual ancestry of Osama bin Laden to thirteenth-century Turkey and the religious leader Taqi al-Din ibn Taymiyya, who developed a very specific understanding of Islam and the role that *jihad* plays in the behavior of believers. Taymiyya believed that Islam required purification from the heresies and corruptions that had crept into it over the six centuries that had elapsed since the death of Muhammad in 632. *Jihad* needed to be made externally against the infidels persecuting Muslims, as well as internally against Muslim rulers who were not sufficiently pure. Basic to his notion of holy war was the belief that only a purified Islam could withstand the power of the nonbelievers.

This was not just an academic exercise for Taymiyya; it was a matter of life and death. At the age of six he had been forced to flee with his family to Damascus in the face of one of the Mongol invasions that swept through the Islamic world in the thirteenth century. These invaders were so cruel and barbaric that no one could withstand them. In 1258, the Mongol commander, a nephew of Genghis Khan, moved against the Abbasid capital of Baghdad, and in a single operation completely razed to the ground one of the finest cities in the civilized world, slaughtering over eight hundred thousand men, women, and children. He took the caliph and his sons out of the city, rolled them inside carpets, and had his horses trample them to death. For Taymiyya, the non-believers were literal enemies and the purity of Islam the only real bulwark against them.

The humiliation of Islam at the hands of the Mongols was rein-forced by humiliation and defeat at the hands of the Europeans. The Crusades during the tenth to the twelfth centuries were bru-tal and cruel, leaving deep wounds and abiding antagonisms. After the defeat of the Ottoman Empire at the gates of Vienna in 1683, European power surged around the world. Islamic civilization, which had peaked during Europe's Dark Ages, was now superceded by a superior military, cultural, political, and eco-nomic force that was just as overwhelming as that of the Mongols, if less barbaric. The Islamic world could only stand by and watch as the Europeans slowly dismembered the Ottoman Empire dur-ing the nineteenth century, with the British and the French finish-ing it off at the end of World War I.

The crowning insult came in 1948 when the state of Israel was established by Western fiat and European Jews were given Arab land in Palestine. As Zbigniew Brzezinski observes, "American involvement in the Middle East is clearly the main impulse of the hatred that has been directed at America. There is no escaping the fact that Arab political emotions have been shaped by the region's encounter with French and British colonialism, by the defeat of the Arab effort to prevent the existence of Israel, and by the sub-sequent American support for Israel and its treatment of the Palestinians, as well as by the direct injection of American power in the region."[4]

Deep in the history of Islam, therefore, is a complex admixture of theology and humiliation at the hands of the infidel so deep that only a holy war against the infidel, combined with a holy war against impurities within Islam itself, will suffice to provide the redemption that the believers know is their just reward. If this were not true, why believe? As the credo of the Muslim Brotherhood states: "God is our objective; the Quran is our constitution; the Prophet is our leader; struggle is our way; and death for the sake of God is the highest of our aspirations."

Coming out of this tradition, and understanding that in a globalizing world networks can be as powerful as nations, Osama bin Laden has been building his army and his tactics for decades with an absolutism that only elevating war to the realm of the holy can instill. He will kill the infidel until he himself is killed. And then, in his place, myriad new Osama bin Ladens will arise, equally committed, equally impassioned, equally ruthless. When you fight fire with fire, the fire is not always vanquished. It can lead instead to a conflagration that burns beyond any borders, particularly if you are fighting a fire that is considered holy and doing so in a world without boundaries.

If we consider that confronting the fundamentalism of bin Laden is the fundamentalism of Hasidism in Israel and the fundamentalism of the Christian right in the United States, and that these strands of religious zeal are replicated throughout these societies in secular displays of patriotism and militarism, it is not easy to be optimistic. For each of these parties, war is both the logical conclusion and the divine affirmation of their dogmatic certainties. If left unbroken, this mutually reinforcing fundamentalism will condemn the Middle East, and elsewhere, to endless cycles of violence and despair.

MOVING BEYOND 9/11   So how do we find our way out of the grip of the fundamentalists? First, we must honor both the grievances of the United States stemming from 9/11 and the grievances of those who carried out the attacks. Only with empathy can either side embrace the complexity of the whole and rise to a more world-centric perspective. Doing so might enable America and the world to tackle another complexity: that the war against the terrorists can only be truly won if a war is also declared on the roots of terrorism: poverty, illiteracy, exploitation, and disease.

Terrorism does not arise in a vacuum. It is rooted in historical, political, social, and economic dysfunctions so deep, so cruel, and so institutionalized that they create and sustain discontent until it spills over into desperation.

As Brzezinski puts it, "Lurking behind every terroristic act is a specific political antecedent. That does not justify either the perpetrator or his political cause. Nonetheless, the fact is that almost all terrorist activity originates from some political conflict and is sustained by it."[5] In other words, unless there is an equally dedicated attack on the *causes* of terrorism, there will never be victory in the *war* against terrorism.

Brzezinski gives several examples of how this can be done. During the 1960s and 1970s, rampant racism in America, expressed through the Ku Klux Klan and other hate groups, was dealt with firmly. The government took action against the groups themselves, put through civil rights legislation, and made sustained efforts to promote civil rights and better race relations. Something similar is being attempted in Northern Ireland today as the British and Irish governments seek a political end to the conflict—so far unsuccessfully but moving in the right direction— and by the Spanish government in the Basque region. Political solutions must accompany firm handling of terrorism for terrorists to be contained.

Tragically, the Bush administration does not appear to have made this connection. It seems content to pour billions of dollars into a desperate fight against the terrorist threat, emphasizing military responses, counterterrorism alliances, and heightened national security precautions. Nowhere in either rhetoric or policy is there any indication that the administration understands the complexities out of which terrorism arises or that addressing simple human needs is the most effective way to induce people to forego violence. The Bush administration, so deeply influenced by the neoconservative and the evangelical Christian worldviews, obsesses over fighting fire with fire while ignoring completely the buckets of water that could actually put out the flames. It is consumed by a Jacksonian impulse for war and vengeance.

The single most important step the American people must take to provide creative leadership in the world is to stop using 9/11 as an excuse for further retributive action. Especially after the invasion of Iraq, the United States must declare that it has had its time of vengeance and that it is now time to move on. The battle against terrorism should no longer be the central pillar and exclusive focus of U.S. government policy. It is time for constructive politics and healing, not more "regime change" in nations the United States does not like.

If out of the trauma of 9/11, Americans can emerge more empathetic to the grievances held by those they now deem terrorists, and if Americans can prove as willing to combat the roots of terrorism as they are the terrorists themselves, then light will have come from the darkness and wisdom will have come from the recesses of hatred and war. America will have learned the wisdom of limits, that in an increasingly complex and interdependent world, no country is an island and no nation has a monopoly on either sorrow or virtue.

9
The Final Empire

TRANSITIONS ARE TIMES OF ACUTE STRESS, disjunction, and upheaval. Apocalyptic visions of the end of the world abound, and values shift like sand in the desert. The old is breaking down and the new is emerging, but the new has not reached sufficient strength to seem reliable or secure. People cling to fundamentalist beliefs, whether religious fundamentalism or market fundamentalism. Periods of transition are thus times of crisis and alienation. Opportunity and abundance can come from such times, but only if there is an invigorating vision of future possibility. Old beliefs and practices must be surrendered and new ways of living and relating embraced, but this requires a strength of spirit and fortitude of mind uncommon in ordinary times.

Leadership during periods of historical turbulence and change is supremely challenging. It must enable the people to abandon what they hold as secure, but which is actually insufficient, and embrace what seems insecure but is potentially sufficient. This can only be done through a vision of the future that instills hope in human possibility. It can only be accomplished with an illumination of light so intense that people surrender their fear of the darkness and are emboldened to take a leap of faith into a new age.

Above all, the United States must articulate a vision of greatness for the twenty-first century. Simply fighting terrorism is not enough. It is a product of fear, not leadership, and thus serves merely as an occasion to exercise military power abroad and erode democracy at home.

What is needed is something decidedly *Wilsonian*, a combination of vision and practical politics that can lift the world again, and in so doing, create a new world order. This is the real challenge ahead. What must be seized is the historical moment of a world in transition from a disjointed amalgamation of nation-states to an integrated global system. What must be confronted are challenges that are global in scope that can only be addressed through a new sense of community and democracy. America needs the next Wilson, the next Roosevelt.

THE ACHIEVEMENTS OF ROOSEVELT AND TRUMAN   The extraordinary leadership of President Franklin Roosevelt and President Truman has been recently chronicled by presidential historian Michael Beschloss in his book *The Conquerors*. He describes how even as Roosevelt was conducting a two-front war against the Axis powers, and at the same time coming to terms with the rapid disintegration of the British Empire, he also began to envision postwar international institutions designed to enhance American power and bring stability to a world he knew America would lead.

Roosevelt, like Wilson before him, was deeply committed to what scholars call the "Grotian tradition," named for Dutch political theorist Hugo Grotius. In the seventeenth century, just as the Enlightenment was getting under way, Grotius asserted that a central aspect of modernity was a "society of states," a group of nations that cohered loosely together under commonly agreed-upon norms and procedures inside the context of a larger system in which anarchy and violence prevailed. Against this society of states, occasional leaders, like Napoleon, would emerge and seek to supercede the common good with a new imperial system. European philosophers and political thinkers spoke out strongly against such tyrants, arguing that they were dangerous and destructive to the community of nations. Such tyrants had to be opposed at all costs.

As noted earlier, resistance to tyranny is a theme that may be traced back to the very beginnings of Western civilization with the resistance of the Greek city-states to Persian imperial expansion. It continued with the opposition by many Romans to the fall of the Roman republic under Julius Caesar. And it continued in more modern form with the Protestant Reformation, the Dutch provinces' struggle against imperial Spain in the sixteenth century, the British development of common law and democratic governance, and from there to the American colonies.

The founding fathers of the United States affirmed the principle of the community of nations, the imperative to oppose authoritarian government, and the importance of honoring prevailing norms of international law. They wanted to secede from Britain, not to supplant it with a radical form of politics, as the Jacobins and Bolsheviks later attempted, but to join the community of nations. As the great American legal scholar James Kent wrote in 1826 in his *Commentaries on American Law:* "When the United States ceased to be a part of the British Empire, and assumed the character of an independent nation, they became subject to that system of rules which reason, morality, and custom had established among the civilized nations of Europe, as their public law."[1]

When the United States emerged as a great power at the start of the twentieth century and American policymakers began to think about the post-British world, there was a general consensus that such a world should be postimperial altogether—that is, a global society of states operating according to democratic and free market principles. In the world those policymakers envisioned, freely elected independent states would supplant the large multinational colonial empires of the Europeans. Free trade would replace their closed imperial economic zones. This was a fundamental principle behind Wilson's proclamations regarding democracy and the League of Nations.

This vision of a postimperial global society of states came to fruition during the Roosevelt administration. In the negotiations of the 1941 Atlantic Charter, which codified the relationship between Great Britain and the United States during World War II, the Americans insisted on Article 3, which declared the "right of all peoples to choose the form of government under which they live." The British sought to have their empire excluded from this clause, but then Under Secretary of State Sumner Wells replied: "If this war is in fact a war for the liberation of peoples, it must assure the sovereign equality of peoples throughout the world, as well as in the world of the Americas. Our victory must bring in its train the liberation of all peoples. Discrimination between peoples because of their race, creed, or color must be abolished. The age of imperialism is ended."[2]

Roosevelt understood that the age of imperialism was indeed over. His genius lay in his commitment to using the national sovereignty of the United States to build a new postimperial system in which sovereign states, equal under international law, could come together to settle disputes through common norms and procedures and take action collaboratively against common challenges. His greatness came when he actually succeeded in replacing the passing British Empire not with another empire, but with a whole new world order.

Roosevelt did this when the United States was arguably even stronger with regard to the rest of the world than it is today and could have much more easily repeated the past than led the way to the future. More than any president of his century, Roosevelt aligned American power with the needs of the time. The result was the empowerment of both American democratic ideals and the community of nations.

While still involved in a great war that engulfed the world, in which American victory seemed probable but was not yet assured, Roosevelt began to plan for the establishment of the United Nations as a permanent diplomatic forum to replace the defunct League of Nations. He knew that his fundamental challenge was to further Wilson's work, which had come out of the first conflict of global dimensions in history. Because World War I had been global, it had generated the first organized attempt at global governance. That was Wilson's great achievement.

But Wilson's League of Nations was neutralized by the refusal of the U.S. Senate to ratify it and by the unfinished business in Europe's imperial drive for power. The Nazis represented continental Europe's final attempt at empire. Theirs was the last spasm of European imperial hubris. Nothing could withstand this storm, and the League of Nations, along with any remaining civility or morality, was swept away. The ensuing Second World War was an even more destructive eruption of violence. It was again a conflict basically among Europeans themselves, but because they controlled colonies all around the world, and because imperial Japan tied its own ambitions to those of the Nazis, drawing in the United States, the conflagration enveloped the whole world.

World War I had unleashed a destructive power that shocked the world. In the first four months of the war, over three hundred thousand Frenchmen alone perished and over six hundred thousand were maimed—almost one-tenth of the republic's males of military age. When the war ended, over ten million lives were lost overall. By the end of World War II, over *fifty* million people had died and countless millions more were wounded, homeless, violated, and dispirited. In both world wars, history had produced new definitions for cruelty, racism, and genocide.

With the default of the League of Nations in mind, President Roosevelt sought to make the United Nations stronger but also more flexible in order to ensure that world war would never again scar the earth. The U.N. was designed to enable the nations to deliberate and work together through the norms and procedures of international law. In terms of its leadership, Roosevelt demanded that the United States have the power to veto any decision the U.N. would make, but he also permitted the other victors of World War II—the Soviet Union, China, France, and Great Britain—to have the veto. Roosevelt died before the war was over, but Truman rose to the occasion and completed the task. The United Nations was established in San Francisco in April 1945, at just about the same time as Adolf Hitler committed suicide in a burned-out bunker in Berlin.

Truman then went on to provide leadership for the creation of the World Bank, the International Monetary Fund, and the other Bretton Woods institutions, which were to provide loans to poor nations and stabilize national currencies while ensuring the financial power of the United States. He granted the other major powers a significant role in the governance and decision making but insisted that there be an 85 percent majority to pass major resolutions. The United States was then guaranteed 17 percent of the votes in the IMF and 18 percent of the votes in the World Bank.

Truman also worked to install a global trade regime that would allow for the continued expansion of the U.S. economy without alienating the nations on which that growth depended. He proposed to Congress an International Trade Organization that would allow developing nations to protect their nascent economies, transfer technologies to poorer countries, and prevent corporations from forming global monopolies. But Congress defeated these proposals.

What finally emerged was the General Agreement on Tariffs and Trade (GATT), which in 1995 was transformed into the World Trade Organization. The GATT was a very imperfect instrument, but it maintained U.S. dominance while allowing for the beginning of multilateral consultations on issues related to world trade. Interestingly, the United States allowed itself to be treated as one nation among others in the WTO, not as an exception, and it consented to be bound by the same tribunals as every other power. In the one area of trade, the United States has surrendered a modicum of sovereignty to a higher power. Under current conditions, this is extraordinary.

Finally, in one of the most majestic acts in all of history, Truman initiated the Marshall Plan, announced in June 1947, which poured billions of U.S. dollars into Europe and Japan to rebuild those regions and resurrect the economies of former enemies. The strategic purpose of the Marshall Plan was to rebuild the nations of Europe and integrate them in a larger political and economic framework. In April 1948, the Organization for European Economic Cooperation (OEEC), precursor to the Organization for Economic Cooperation and Development (OECD), was created with the mandate to coordinate European economic and social policy.

Combined with a willingness to use American military power to protect the free world from the Soviet threat—a willingness that Truman affirmed through the establishment of NATO in

1949—the actions of Roosevelt and Truman generated and framed the world order that emerged from the ashes of the Second World War. It was America at its finest moment, using its national sovereignty to consolidate its own power and at the same time establish the international institutions necessary for the common good. It was a near-perfect execution of American military, economic, and political power.

Roosevelt and Truman thereby succeeded in advancing the dream of the Enlightenment: a society of states operating under common norms and international law. They did this while enhancing American power but not falling prey to Napoleonic temptations. They designed a framework for international deliberations, the globalization of market economies, and the spread of democratic governance. Like the philosopher kings of Rome, these two presidents used the national power of the center for the good of the periphery, and both prospered. They combined a new strategic vision with institutions that established and governed a new world order.

The Soviet Union tried to challenge the United States by repeating the age-old pattern of highly militarized and authoritarian imperial control over vassal states in eastern Europe and central Asia. Essentially, the Soviets sought to perpetuate the colonialism of the past. The Soviet Union became artificially and temporarily strong because it developed nuclear weapons, but by 1991 it fell largely of its own weight. Only the United States created the future: an open system of commerce and justice, which it dominated to be sure, but which was based on the principles of international law, free market economics, and democratic governance and which invited other nations to become independent, prosperous, and free.

In this context, Jean Monnet was able to establish the beginnings of the European Union. Like the Americans, he too combined light with power. He provided the Europeans with a bold new strategic purpose as well as the technical means to allow them to integrate and prosper. Even as the Marshall Plan combined restoration of national sovereignty with the integration of the European nations inside the OEEC, so Monnet inspired the establishment of the Coal and Steel Commission in the context of a new European unity. This combination of strategic purpose and technical means, over time, led to the creation of the European Union and the extraordinary achievement of unity in a region that had been ravaged by wars for two millennia.

Today, there is an international consensus in favor of democracy, some version of open markets, and the development of international norms, rules, and procedures inside the U.N. system. It is not a perfect system but it still represents an extraordinary advance over colonialism. The U.N. has been far more successful than the League of Nations was. This advance has taken place because of the inherent power of these ideas and because they were championed by the United States, which used its national sovereignty to actualize them at a crucial moment of choice.

Choices matter. When leaders choose, they shape the nation. And when America chooses, it shapes the world. This is what President Bush did when he defined the aftermath of 9/11 as a "war." Roosevelt, too, had declared war, using Pearl Harbor in a very Jacksonian way. Literally within weeks of that attack, the United States was in total war with the Japanese and soon found itself fighting for its life on two fronts simultaneously. The country had never before been so threatened. Imperial Japan came at the United States with everything it had. It was every bit as ferocious in the Pacific as the Nazis were in Europe. Roosevelt mobilized the entire nation for war with the same drive and success he had demonstrated in pulling it out of the Great Depression. It was a total effort that, in the end, consumed his life. His greatness lay in his ability to balance the Jacksonian impulse to protect with the Wilsonian commitment to build. Thus he won the war as well as winning the peace.

New Global Challenges   It is in the spirit of Wilson, Roosevelt, and Truman that the United States should now provide global leadership. It must do this through the three pillars of its greatness discussed in chapter 3: economic power, democratic idealism, and military strength. All three, taken together, brought it to world supremacy. All three, taken separately, must now be reworked and applied in new ways, appropriate to an integrating world.

Looking to the future, what this means is that the United States must lead in providing for the global security of the international community. This includes taking seriously the challenges presented by failed and failing states and the need to solve international threats by creating new cooperative structures. As it exercises its dominion, the United States must recognize that there is in fact another superpower: world public opinion, which it must respect and deal with creatively. The United States must work at the global level to ensure that private gain is regulated within the context of the common good. It must support network democracy and global issue networks as the key ingredients to establishing democracy at the global level. And, above all, the United States must ensure that an effective global governance regime is established before, not after, the global catastrophe that will inevitably ensue if we do not solve the problems at hand.

PROVIDING GLOBAL SECURITY FOR THE INTERNATIONAL COMMUNITY

Any notion of a community of nations, or a society of states, must begin with providing for its security. If there is no security, there is no peace. If there is no peace, then democracy, freedom, and commerce cannot flourish. In the immediate future, the United States must be the guarantor of this security. It is the only nation with the resources and power to do so, and in the end, this is the most fundamental requisite of empire.

As noted earlier, President Monroe proclaimed the Monroe Doctrine in 1823, declaring that the Western Hemisphere was off-limits to foreign powers. In 1949, President Truman extended the Monroe Doctrine to Europe in deed if not in word, declaring that region within the national security domain of the United States and therefore off-limits to Soviet encroachment. This commitment was codified by the establishment of NATO.

In 2002, President Bush declared that the United States would not tolerate any competing power anywhere in the world and would act preemptively to protect U.S. interests. Thus U.S. troops invaded Iraq and seized the Tigris-Euphrates river basin to demonstrate this power and prerogative. In effect, President Bush extended the Monroe Doctrine to the world: the entire planet is now within America's national security domain.

The United States now has a basic choice to make: will it merely seek to consolidate long-term military dominance over the planet? Or will it lead the world, in the spirit of a true transitional empire, and use its military primacy—as Roosevelt and Truman did—to enforce a political agenda that will give rise to the next generation of international norms and the global institutions needed for world security?

The misfortune of the U.S. invasion of Iraq is that because it was executed in a fit of Jacksonian pique, the United States broke the very laws and procedures that undergird the community of nations and therefore constitute an essential part of world security. In seeking its own national security, the Bush administration undermined common security. It broke trust with the nations and used its military might in defiance of the nations. This will take time and careful tending to remedy, but it must be done, for quite literally, the future security of the world is at stake.

Over the short term, the world will face increasing turbulence in the security domain for two fundamental reasons. First, the United States is not yet prepared to use its military on behalf of the common good; and second, the endemic crises in the international order are growing worse. Although the United States will undoubtedly attempt to work within the context of U.N. resolutions and the broader framework and constraints of international law when possible, it is not likely to be impeded by them when they do not coincide with its interests. And this will lead to even greater turbulence in the international system because it will violate the central norm of modernity: the community of nations.

The emerging policy of establishing "coalitions of the willing" implies ad hoc partnerships for changing occasions. This almost certainly will have the effect of broadening American alliances beyond the Euro-American axis that has been the cornerstone of American policies and actions for much of the past. NATO, like the U.N., has limited geostrategic utility.

This situation became clear in Iraq. The coalition that backed the United States in that invasion—which included some Europeans but not others—was a precursor of things to come. In the future, NATO and the U.N. are likely to become increasingly marginalized, and other major countries like China, India, Russia, and the U.K., along with smaller countries such as Poland, Israel, and Turkey, will emerge as part of the U.S. alliance structure.

In a globalizing world, coalitions of the willing may come from new and unexpected quarters, as will enemies and abstainers. Alliances and threats, friends and foes, common ground and battle lines will shift quickly, constantly, and unpredictably. Policing the world as the neoconservatives envision, will be fraught with problems under every conceivable scenario. Replacing support for the community of nations with the development of coalitions of the willing is inherently dangerous because it sets in motion an inherently unstable equilibrium. Over time, the strategy of coalitions of the willing will weaken the United States because it will undermine international stability.

There is an even greater danger. The most serious challenge to U.S. military power arises in the fact that the security needs of the world are not the areas in which the U.S. military currently excels. The United States has an awesome capacity to attack and conquer, but what is really needed is nation building and peacekeeping in failed and failing states. The U.S. military is primed for war against aggressive nations, but the real security crises are in nations that are disintegrating from within and cannot even function as nations.

The U.S. military and intelligence communities are currently shifting their tactics to enable them to deal with the terrorism that grows out of these failed states. But as we saw in chapter 8, the war on terrorism cannot succeed unless there is an equally profound commitment to eradicate the roots of terrorism. Terrrorism is a political and cultural challenge, not simply a military one. In effect, the vast U.S. military forces around the world will have to become as much peacekeepers as warriors, as much nation builders as destroyers of rogue states if global security is to be assured. This reality challenges the Pentagon's current policy, which precludes U.S. troops from being used for peacekeeping.

The magnitude of the security problem confronting the United States can be seen in the fact that roughly one-third of all states in the world over which it now exercises military dominion are what

the IMF calls "underperforming"—a euphemism for failing and
failed states. Several billion people spread across the global south
are included in this statistic. Failing and failed states, and the
problems they embody, represent the single most critical challenge to American security and global stability.

Here's a quick calculus: at the end of World War II there were
seventy-four independent nations in the world; by 1950 there
were eighty-nine. By 1995, there were 192 of them, with the
largest increase coming in the 1960s, mainly in Africa, where
twenty-five new nations were established between 1960 and 1964,
and in the early 1990s, where they emerged mainly in eastern
Europe. Also notable is that eighty-seven of the current members
of the United Nations have populations of less than 5 million, fifty-
eight have fewer than 2.5 million, and thirty-five have less than
500,000. In other words, more than half of the independent
nations of the world in 2002 had fewer inhabitants than the state of
Massachusetts.

Most of the recent nations have been established at a time of
major transition in the global economy and political landscape.
The collapse of authoritarian regimes in Latin America and East
Asia in the 1980s, coupled with the collapse of the Soviet Union in
1991 and the rapid formation of independent states across central
Asia, in addition to the former Soviet client states in eastern
Europe, gave rise to a plethora of nations in transition and in need
of fundamental assistance in building their nations anew along
democratic and free market lines. This comes on top of the dozens
of African states, established in the 1960s and 1970s, that need the
same support. Unable to make the transition successfully, many
have succumbed to internal conflict, corruption, and social disintegration.

A World Bank study of fifty-two conflicts since 1960 found that
wars begun after 1980 lasted three times longer than those begun
before 1980. Sudan is a classic case of a failed state; its civil war
goes back over two decades, there have been over two million
casualties as a result, and there is little prospect for a solution. Not
surprisingly, Sudan is a haven for the international terrorist
network.

Contributing to these state failures are the deleterious effects of globalization and the neoliberal policies of the international financial institutions, as noted in chapter 2. Violence and social disorder are also linked to rapid population growth. In the next twenty years the human population will increase by another two billion people, reaching some eight billion by 2020. Some of the most dramatic growth will take place in the Middle East— Afghanistan, Pakistan, Saudi Arabia, and Yemen—all Islamic nations with strong anti-American and anti-Western sentiments.

Only sub-Saharan Africa, already rife with failing states, will face a demographic challenge even more acute than that of the Middle East. There, the pandemic of HIV AIDS will continue to combine with the high birth rates and threaten internal disintegration and governmental collapse, creating another perfect haven for terrorist networks as well as criminals generally.

Failed states in turn threaten their orderly neighbors through the inevitable migration of displaced peoples seeking escape. This in turn creates lucrative markets in illegal workers, the sex trade, and the trade in body organs. There is now more south-south migration than south-north migration, and it is almost entirely due to instability in failed and failing states throughout the swath of degrading poverty that spans the global south.

If it attempts to seek military solutions to all the security crises that are certain to erupt from these failed and failing states, the United States will certainly collapse under the effort. Kosovo and Bosnia provide examples of excruciatingly difficult political and social situations that defied short-term solutions, and this was true even though the United States alone spent nearly $15 billion on military intervention in the region between 1991 and 2000. Expenditures for the actual invasion of Iraq are estimated at well over $200 billion. Yet there are dozens of potential Kosovos and Iraqs out there—that's what failing states breed.

What is occurring in Afghanistan after the removal of the Taliban and the regime change in Iraq provides another cautionary tale. In response to 9/11, the United States took the initiative to overthrow the Taliban in Afghanistan. After gaining approval from the U.N. Security Council to do so, the U.S. military, working with a small but committed number of European and other forces, eliminated the Taliban and brought Afghanistan's Northern Alliance to power. Working together, the United States, the U.N., and the EU shepherded in the new government of Hamid Karzai, and the task of rebuilding Afghanistan began. So far, so good.

But then a strange thing happened. While President Bush and Secretary of State Powell called for a Marshall Plan reminiscent of Truman and committed the United States to extensive reconstruction, in fact Washington pledged a meager $296 million and actually fought off congressional leaders who wanted to put in more aid. Bush's budget director, Mitch Daniels, told congressional leaders who wanted to allocate $150 million for agricultural and educational assistance in Afghanistan that they would get no more than $40 million. During 2002 and 2003, the United States spent about $1 billion a month on military operations there and only $25 million a month in reconstruction aid. In addition, no American troops are allowed to be used for peacekeeping purposes.

The net result has been that other nations have been equally parsimonious with their resources and troops. Not surprisingly, Afghanistan, despairing of long-term U.S. involvement, is increasingly falling back into the hands of the warlords. During 2003, many humanitarian agencies closed their Afghan operations because of civil violence. President Karzai has been relegated by the growing power of the warlords to little more than mayor of Kabul. And, amazingly, President Bush's primary purpose all along—to defeat al-Qaeda—seems to have been forgotten, for the Taliban and al-Qaeda are still operating in both Afghanistan and neighboring Pakistan. Afghanistan is deconstructing as much as it is reconstructing, leaving the United States with a legacy there of quick victory in war, followed by a confused and bloody peace.

The United States did not focus on serious reconstruction in Afghanistan because it had no broader strategic mission other than to defeat the terrorists militarily. Without this larger vision, the United States quickly lost interest and moved on to the next military venture—Iraq—because this fit with the neoconservative view of the war against terrorism. If President Bush had been more Wilsonian, he would have focused as much on reconstruction as on regime change. The promised Marshall Plan would have happened and the United States would have demonstrated as much leadership in establishing the peace as it has in gaining victory in war.

Instead, it was left to the Europeans and the United Nations to take on the brunt of the relief work in Afghanistan, the coordination of the development aid, and the long-term nation building. By the end of 2002, there were as many non-American as American troops in the country, and the European Union, working in close relationship with U.N. agencies, had borne most of the costs of the Afghan reconstruction. Whereas the Bush administration failed to live up to its promises, the international community, led by the Europeans and the U.N., rose to the occasion as best they could given the limitations of American vision and resources.

Afghanistan is not unique. The Europeans and the United Nations, supported to some extent by the United States, have in the last five years engaged in nation-building exercises in Bosnia, Cambodia, East Timur, and Kosovo, all in different combinations and with different outcomes but generally enough to keep the situation from further disintegration. The United States is now actively engaged in nation building in Iraq but with limited U.N. and European support, largely because it invaded essentially alone and has no other choice but to bear the reconstruction costs proportionally alone. In addition, it has made it clear that the United States and the United States alone will redesign the Iraqi government, economy, and military. The costs of this policy are running at $4 billion per month and constitute a serious fiscal challenge even to the United States. As in Afghanistan, Iraq challenges the United States with political problems generated by continued guerilla subversion and economic instability.

The point of these sorry tales is that without a larger worldview, without a larger vision reminiscent of Wilson or Roosevelt or Truman, the international community, ever deepening in turbulence, will hobble along from one crisis to another without direction, without the necessary resources, and most fundamentally, without American leadership. When we consider Rischard's point, that there are at least twenty other equally urgent challenges facing the world community in addition to failed states, we get a measure of what *generative crisis* really means.

In terms of the specific case of nation building, what is currently an ad hoc case-by-case stumbling of the United States and the international community from one crisis to the next must be transformed. The critical task of nation building must be institutionalized. The failures of Afghanistan and the U.S. overextension in Iraq provide an ideal opportunity for the United States and the international community to come together to gather information, develop options, and make recommendations, which might include setting up a new "International Reconstruction Fund" specifically dedicated to deal with nation building.

Sebastian Mallaby, editorial writer and columnist for the *Washington Post,* suggests that if this new institution were designed along the model of the World Bank or IMF, it could be the same hybrid type of organization: embodying American leadership while also being multinational.[3] The mixed records of these institutions should not obscure their organizational strengths, he says. They are staffed by highly educated professionals from around the world, are less driven by national patronage than are agencies of the United Nations, and have shown themselves to be adaptable to changing world situations.

Such an institution could be established in the context of but outside the direct jurisdiction of the United Nations, thus sparing it from the constraints of the U.N. Security Council, with its system of vetoes, or the rigidities of the U.N. General Assembly, with its one country, one vote system of deliberation. Furthermore, if besides the professional pool of talent currently available from the governmental sector, the new institution included expertise and knowledge from the NGO community and the business sector, and if it worked with agencies and community-based organizations in the target countries rather than just with governments, it could actually be effective in the emerging global context.

This new International Reconstruction Fund could be set up and financed initially by the wealthiest countries in the OECD and the other nations that currently contribute to the World Bank's subsidized lending program. The new fund would need resources, expertise, and political clout, and possibly troops at its disposal. Its mandate would be to assemble a nation-building capacity robust enough to deal with this critical global issue, and it would be deployed however and wherever its board decided. The begging and arm twisting that characterizes current peacekeeping and nation-building efforts could be things of the past. As Mallaby puts it:

> Summoning such leadership is immensely difficult, but America and its allies have no easy options in confronting failed states. They cannot wish away the problem that chaotic power vacuums can pose. They cannot fix it with international institutions as they currently exist. And they cannot sensibly wish for a unilateral American imperium. They must either mold the international machinery to address the problems of their times, as their predecessors did in creating the U.N., the World Bank, and the IMF after World War II. Or they can muddle along until some future collection of leaders rises to the challenge.[4]

SOLVING INTERNATIONAL THREATS WITH NEW COOPERATIVE STRUCTURES

It is at this juncture that a deeper question concerning world security must be asked: What should the United States and the world do when the next Saddam Hussein emerges, clever enough to consolidate state control and yet wicked enough to warrant international action? How should the United States lead and the world respond to the next Hitler, or the next rogue leader?

An excellent suggestion on this question was made by Anne-Marie Slaughter, dean of the Woodrow Wilson School of Public and International Affairs, in the aftermath of the Iraq war.[5] She suggested that rather than marginalizing the U.N. and going it alone with "coalitions of the willing," the U.S. government should provide leadership in persuading the Security Council to reexamine how it defines threats to international security that are sufficient to require the use of force. Slaughter's recommendation is that the human rights side of the U.N. be linked with the security side and a set of criteria developed to guide the U.N. and the

Security Council when such situations arise. The U.N. already has a substantial body of work and a set of agreements devoted to propagating and enforcing human rights laws and holding governments accountable for torturing, repressing, and killing their people. It also has a substantial body of work dedicated to the regulation and diminution of armed conflict. It would be entirely within its mandate, therefore, for the U.N. to develop a set of threshold conditions that, when violated, would automatically trigger a discussion about the use of force.

Slaughter proposed three criteria: possession of weapons of mass destruction, grave and systematic violations of human rights, and evidence of aggressive intent with regard to neighboring nations. If these three conditions were all met, the Security Council would consider the use of force in eliminating the threat. It would thus have clear criteria and it would have a mandate to consider superceding specific national sovereignties for the sake of the common good.

There is a larger issue, too: how the United States and the world community can help protect people in countries whose governments are either unable or unwilling to take corrective action in the face of humanitarian disasters. Weapons of mass destruction are certainly critical challenges, but so is ethnic cleansing.

This issue was taken up by the International Commission on Intervention and State Sovereignty, initiated by then–Canadian Foreign Minister Lloyd Axworthy. In its findings, released in December 2001, the commission pointed out that there were no agreed-upon rules for handling cases such as Somalia, Rwanda, and Kosovo. Both U.S. and U.N. action was in most cases widely considered to be too little too late, and then misconceived, poorly resourced, or badly executed.

The commission pointed out that humanitarian disasters, mass killings, economic dislocation, development of weapons of mass destruction are becoming endemic problems that will seriously destabilize the world if not handled effectively. Institutional capacities must be built to deal with them through commonly agreed-upon norms and procedures. It is clear that the United States cannot deal with all these security issues either on its own through its military might or with "coalitions of the willing." These monumental challenges can only be dealt with through international cooperation, with criteria and conditions established for the United States and the community of nations in order to act legitimately and decisively together.

The commission argued that if the international community is to respond to these challenges, "the whole debate must be turned on its head. The issue must be reframed not as an argument about the 'right to intervene' but about the 'responsibility to protect.'"[6] All sovereign states must acknowledge this responsibility and the international community must take it up when they do not. This implies a duty to react not just when there are national security situations but also when there is a compelling need to protect human life.

The commission suggested that early warning systems be put in place and preventive measures be taken before the crises become acute. Military intervention should be the last resort and only take place if civilians are faced with massive loss of life, such as when genocide is clearly occurring or about to occur. It should take place only in the context of several precautionary principles: if it is based on the right intention, meaning that the motive has to be to halt or avert human suffering, if it uses proportional means, and if there are reasonable prospects for success.

Coming up with the definitive answers to these complex questions is the task of the Security Council. Acknowledging that they exist and asking why the United States is not taking the leadership in demanding that the international community grapple with these questions is the point here. The issue is American leadership, or the lack of it, on the real security issues of the day, and especially in regard to the United Nations, which was specifically founded by the United States to help build, define, and legitimize the authority of the international community.

The U.N. was set up as a framework within which the member states could negotiate agreements and establish norms of behavior for the community of nations in which Roosevelt and the Europeans believed so strongly. The authority of the United Nations, therefore, does not rest so much on coercive power as on its capacity to bestow or withdraw legitimacy. It is the symbol and guarantor of international law and universal norms. Those who thwart its authority not only lose credibility themselves, as President Bush did when he invaded Iraq without U.N. approval, but undermine the one institution mandated to ensure international stability and the rule of law.

The fact that the Security Council failed to act in both Kosovo and Iraq seriously damaged its legitimacy and power. The task of the future, however, should not be to ignore or replace the United Nations but to make it work more effectively. Indeed, all international organizations need to be strengthened and better financed. The edifice of international law and the body of work that seeks to articulate universal norms are very fragile and easily thwarted. If a great power such as the United States undermines these principles, anarchy and chaos will be the predictable results. Sooner or later, the United States itself is certain to be victimized by the very weakness in the international system it is now causing by undermining and bypassing the United Nations and the international law it represents.

RECOGNIZING TODAY'S OTHER SUPERPOWER: WORLD PUBLIC OPINION

The great irony confronting the United States is that while it has more military power than any empire in history, it also is more constrained in the use of that power than any empire has ever been. This is not only because of the growing body of international laws and procedures within which it must act, but because the very nature of violence and politics has changed. This is the essential point made by Jonathan Schell in his book *The Unconquerable World.* Iraq notwithstanding, military might simply does not have the utility it once did.

In the first half of the twentieth century, with the rise of fascism and communism and the experience of two world wars, there was violence at unprecedented levels. In his book *Out of Control,* Zbigniew Brzezinski asserts that there was more violence during that part of the twentieth century than during the rest of human history combined. The American military behemoth was fashioned during those violent days.

The advent of nuclear weapons in 1945 took the magnitude of potential violence into the realm of the unimaginable, threatening the very survival of the human species. However, possessing such weapons of mass destruction had the paradoxical effect of actually paralyzing the military power of the United States and the Soviet Union, which during the Cold War were locked in a spiraling arms race. Under the threat of mutual assured destruction, the use of violence actually abated. There were, of course, numerous wars and conflicts during the second half of the twentieth century, but nothing to compare with the carnage of the first half. It was during this period that America was defeated in Vietnam and the Soviets routed in Afghanistan.

Simultaneously, another kind of power was rising, what Vaclav Havel calls the *power of the powerless.* This was the emerging influence of civil society and the effectiveness of citizen action around the world. Building on the labor and suffragette movements of the late nineteenth and early twentieth centuries, there was a veritable explosion in citizen activism after World War II, initially for national self-determination and nuclear disarmament and then for human rights, the environment, feminism, globalization, and a whole spectrum of issues related to social equity and justice. The power of nongovernmental organizations (NGOs), interacting and connecting with each other and with the government and private sectors, also emerged. And so as the United States was emerging as the world's sole superpower, the world's first global social movement was also taking shape and exerting its influence.

Schell recounts that it was the Polish activist Adam Michnik who said in the 1970s that peaceful resistance to Soviet domination of eastern Europe was more powerful than the atomic bomb. And it was the activism of the citizens in that region, combined with relentless military pressure from the United States and NATO, that liberated first Poland and then the rest of eastern Europe from Soviet control. In 1989, the power of the people succeeded where the power of the military could not: the Berlin Wall was torn down, and in 1991, the Soviet Union dissolved.

During the same period in the United States, the civil rights, environmental, feminist, and social justice movements compelled new legislation and reforms across a range of areas and concerns. Similar movements took shape in Europe, and more recently, have taken shape across the global south. The result is a global lattice-work of citizen activism that scrutinizes government policies and actions, challenges economic and political priorities, and recommends social reform and environmental protection across a spectrum of areas.

What does all this mean? The United States is exercising its military power in a world system in which there are now *two* superpowers: the United States and world public opinion. This is what confronted the United States in Iraq: the voices of local peoples all around the world joining together to state their opposition to the war, especially without the approval of the United Nations. In the future, international civil society could play the balancing role that in previous eras was played by competing imperial powers.

As a result, U.S. military power must increasingly cause fewer and fewer civilian casualties. This is the aim of American military technology. It is also the demand of the international community. With reporters now "embedded" in U.S. military units and television coverage instant and worldwide, everything the U.S. military does and will do in the future will be scrutinized as never before by an increasingly well-informed and critical international public. This will be so even if the media in the United States itself becomes ever more compliant under government manipulation.

Because the international community is so highly politicized, the more the United States acts unilaterally and resorts to force, the more it will be mistrusted. And the more the United States is mistrusted, the weaker its political influence will be. In Iraq, America succeeded in removing Saddam Hussein from power but lost the war for international public support. America will experience a tragedy of Athenian proportions if in the face of decreasing political effectiveness it resorts to increasing use of force.

The old adage says, "Covenants without swords are but words." But it is also true that swords without covenants produce disloyalty. Appreciating both these truths, the Romans were able to convert their military might into a lasting political dominion. Similarly, Roosevelt and Truman were able to defeat fascism and build a new world order. In the future, the United States must commit itself to building cooperative structures if it is to win the hearts and minds of people around the world. People will respect American military power if they simultaneously can count on American leadership to help them solve their problems.

At the local level, this means the United States must support the creation of civil society rather than political violence and intimidation. At the national level, it means supporting democracy rather than backing authoritarian and corrupt regimes. At the international level, it means working within multilateral frameworks wherever possible rather than disregarding them for the sake of unilateral advantage.

Put simply, for U.S. military power to have a lasting effect as well as international support, it must be exercised within a context of cooperation. For American power to be effective, the extension of law must follow the victory of its armies and the construction of cooperative institutions must parallel the buildup of its armaments. Rogue regimes may be susceptible to military overthrow, but the deeper issues—such as global warming, ozone depletion, poverty, or HIV AIDS—cannot be solved by cruise missiles or by Bradley Fighting Vehicles.

These challenges will only be solved by cooperative action across borders, supported by the citizens, and done in the name of the community of nations. The purpose of American power must not be to dominate the nations but to empower the community of nations. This is what it means to say that the challenge of America is to be a transitional empire. It must be a superpartner as much as a superpower.

REGULATING PRIVATE GAIN IN THE CONTEXT OF THE GLOBAL COMMON GOOD

The same logic pertains in the economic sphere, where America is almost as strong as it is militarily. Although its military dominance is the more obvious, its corporate dominance is the more pervasive. Of the one hundred largest economies in the world, fifty-one are corporations. Of these fifty-one corporations, forty-seven are American.

If in military matters the United States seems intent on retaining the prerogative to act unilaterally with coalitions of the willing, in commerce the United States will continue, in its own self-interest, to bring as many nations as possible into the free market system and the multilateral frameworks of economic globalization. Multilateralism has been and will continue to be the objective of U.S. economic policy. As the first nonterritorial empire, the United States will continue its historic mission of creating free market economies and free trade zones everywhere it can in order to ensure a global harvest for its corporations.

But even as military ventures will have to take note of world opinion and be complemented by institution building in order to be effective, so the key for sustained American economic power will be to frame free market economics in an equally compelling political commitment to social equity. To recall the point made earlier by George Soros, markets are amoral. Unregulated, they lead to dynamic prosperity and extraordinary wealth. Unregulated, they also lead to inordinate social inequities and environmental devastation. Global leadership is necessary to ensure that there is a moral context for the markets, which is currently a missing ingredient in both U.S. economic policy and the WTO regulations. As Soros puts it: "We have global markets but we do not have a global society. And we cannot build a global society without taking into account moral considerations."[7]

This means that the WTO must be reformed, and the process of building compensatory institutions at a global level begun in earnest. For example, the free market in America is heavily regulated by the Securities and Exchange Commission, the Federal Trade Commission, the Federal Communications Commission, the Federal Drug Administration, and myriad other national, state, and local bodies. No such institutions exist at a global level, which is one of the reasons why there are so many critical global problems. Unregulated markets cause havoc in society, devastation in the environment, and manic behavior in the financial markets and world economy. Because the United States learned these truths, especially after the Great Depression of 1929, it built those institutions internally. They have been essential to the fair regulation of American capitalism.

However, just as building cooperative structures in the security domain should not mean a lessening of military force, neither should creating regulatory global institutions mean the denigration of free market economics. Soros, the ultimate capitalist, is clear on this: "The difference between global capitalism and a global open society is not so great. It is not an either/or alternative but merely a change of emphasis, a better balance between competition and cooperation, a reassertion of morality amid our amoral preoccupations."[8]

Soros's view is consistent with those held by the father of modern capitalism, Adam Smith. Smith wrote two books on subjects that in his mind were interrelated: *The Theory of Moral Sentiments* and *The Wealth of Nations*. In the first book, he set forth the commonly held view of the Enlightenment—that happiness is the greatest value and that one becomes happy by making others happy. His contemporary, David Hume, along with Jeremy Bentham and John Stuart Mill, developed this into the theory of utilitarianism—that governance in society should strive for the greatest good for the greatest number.

In *The Wealth of Nations*, Smith worked out the implications of the first theory in the economic sphere. For him, consumption is the sole end and purpose of production. This was not a matter of opinion for him, but a matter of natural law. The interests of the producers of goods and services should only be assisted by the state insofar as they satisfy the consumers. For him, competition and free choice among consumers form the basis of the free market, not competition between the producers, or as we know them, the corporations. In Smith's view, the companies are only there to satisfy consumer needs. This is what, for him, contributes to the common good and the happiness of all: producers should serve the needs of the people. The people are made happy when their needs are met, and the producers receive a profit from this service. True capitalism, therefore, links the production of wealth with the needs of the common good.

In the United States, the relationship between producers and consumers has been turned on its head and the link between the generation of wealth and the requisites for the common good broken. As a result, full rights have been given to corporations, while only grudgingly, and in a very limited way, have they been given to consumers. Profit has been elevated above the satisfaction of human needs. But in the beginning, and as originally envisioned, this was not so. The common good was the context for wealth, not the servant and potential victim.

Bringing these two elements together again at a global level means radically reforming not just the World Trade Organization but also the IMF, the World Bank, and the numerous multinational agencies sculpted to serve neoliberal principles. It also means creating global institutions that have parity with them and can modulate them. Right now, the issue of trade is given primacy over every other issue, and therefore, the international financial institutions are given priority over any other international organization and regulatory frameworks.

To ensure social equity, organizations such as the International Labor Organization, which coordinates labor laws, should be given peer status with these international financial institutions. To protect the environment, a Global Environmental Organization to coordinate the plethora of environmental issues and laws must be established. There is a host of other areas in which new institutions and mechanisms need to be created to manage the global system.

The essential challenge is to create a series of checks and balances at the global level so that trade, investments, and currency flows are regulated in the context of abiding concern for the welfare of people and the protection of the environment. Private gain, whether at the local, national, or global levels, must be framed by the public good for people to prosper. Otherwise, neither the public good nor private gain will long endure.

As in the security domain, the question concerning global economic reform is this: Where will the leadership come from? Soros is correct when he says:

> The initiative has to come from the United States. It requires a profound change of attitude, a veritable change of heart. Such a radical change is not possible in normal times, but these are not normal times. We have become aware how precarious our civilization is. It does not make sense to devote all our energies to improving our relative position in a social

system when the system itself is drifting toward disaster. The United States is the only country in the world that is in a position to initiate a change in the world order, to replace the Washington consensus with a global open society. To do so we must abandon the unthinking pursuit of narrow self-interest and give some thought to the future of humanity.[9]

SUPPORTING NETWORK DEMOCRACY AND GLOBAL ISSUE NETWORKS

The subject of global economic reform leads to one final issue. Giving primacy to trade is easy. Establishing social equity takes place at an entirely different level of complexity. It is here that the problems are increasingly acute, the power of the state critically deficient, and the need for a radically new notion of governance urgent. Paradoxically, it is at this level that the redesign of the system of nation-states into a global system could begin.

Addressing the crisis of the nation-state system can only be accomplished by redefining democracy at a global level. What is required at the level of the problems arising from cultural clashes, ethnic conflicts, systemic poverty, social alienation, and the global environment is not merely more money or more outmoded pre-globalization attitudes and techniques. What is required is a new form of democracy. It is at this level that the redesign of the world system could begin, and it is at this level that the United States, the carrier of the Athenian impulse, could most dramatically lead the way. In an integrating world, the first global democratic empire must pioneer the meaning of *network governance*. Network governance is the gateway to democracy at the global level and therefore to the effective management of the global system.

World government is not the solution nor is it a political possibility under current conditions. The world does not need yet another level of bureaucracy and more stultifying processes of deliberation. The experience of the European Union, as grand as the idea of integration is, or of the U.N., as elevated as its commitment to the community of nations, does not inspire replication. In an integrating world, *governance,* not *government,* is the key to effective management of the global system because *networks,* not *nations,* are the emergent powers of the future.

If we recall the twenty global challenges listed by Rischard—ranging from global warming to HIV AIDS to tax evasion—what is common among them all is that the current system of nation-states cannot solve them. As a result, all of them have become chronic and many have become acute. To deal with virtually all of these problems, says Rischard, *global issue networks* should be created. This would minimize complication and hierarchy, help deal with the challenges in a timely and effective way, and create a latticework of networked governance through which governments, civil society, and the business community could come together in communities of shared mission.

Global issue networks would amplify the role of government by bringing in the creativity, intelligence, and capacities of the private sector. The key to transforming the nation-state system is not to abolish nation-states but to make them more effective. Sovereignty should not be denigrated but redefined at a global level, using the institutions already in place and adding to their capacities from the private sector. This redefinition means that at the global level, sovereignty increasingly rests with networks, not just with nations.

Rischard suggests three stages to the formation of global issue networks. First, there would be a *constitutional phase* in which the network is convened and set in motion. Each network would comprise national governments and international institutions, the relevant expert groups from civil society, and business firms with relevant expertise. The representative from the governmental sector would lead the network with a representative each from the civil society and business sectors. Together, they would select members of the network, choosing those organizations and specialists with the most knowledge and expertise in dealing with their particular problem. The network would initially comprise dozens, and over time, hundreds of groups working together from many different disciplines and from around the world. Networks would work with other networks as issues overlap and recommendations coincide.

After each network is convened, or formed, the second, *norm-producing phase* would begin. This phase would deal with knowledge aggregation: evaluating the size and dimensions of the problem, producing alternatives and options, and finally, reaching consensus on recommendations and norms. During this process, extensive electronic town meetings would be held, in which all interested parties could contribute ideas and information and participate in "deliberative polling" to clarify areas of agreement and disagreement and reach consensus.

The third and final phase, the *implementation phase,* would then begin, in which the network would seek to get its norms and recommendations adopted by national governments and international institutions on a voluntary basis. Norms are not legislation, says Rischard; the networks would not have regulatory authority over governments, business, or civil society. Rather, the challenge would be to use moral persuasion and publicity to get countries to change behavior, adopt guidelines, and enact policies.

The tragedy of the current situation is that while governments are struggling relentlessly but futilely along on their own trying to solve global problems, there are literally thousands of NGOs and businesses with the expertise and commitment to help. But the current system of nation-states essentially precludes them from playing a meaningful role. If given the sanction of a power such as the United States government, global issue networks would have the benefit of speed, legitimacy, and diversity. They would build on the current institutions and governmental bodies. They would actually begin to solve global problems, while at the same time revitalizing the meaning of democracy at a global level.

The suggestion that American leadership be applied to developing network governance may seem radical and far-fetched, particularly given its current preoccupation with national security and the war on terrorism. But in addition to being what is crucially needed, it is completely consistent with American history and ideals. American democracy has always been radical. While European democracy generally contextualizes the individual within the context of society, which is what gives European culture its more communal ethos, America was birthed with the notion that government should be limited by the rights of the individual. The individual is sovereign in America, the government contained. This is perhaps the most radical interpretation of democracy ever developed. Bringing the two notions together is the key to the future of democracy, whether at the national or global levels.

This is where we can discern echoes of Atlantis. Given the strands of American history and the reasons given earlier for its emergence as the world's superpower, it is completely consistent, even necessary for its continued power in the world, that, along with overwhelming, even ruthless military might and a deeply commercial, even exploitative view of the world, the United States should also continue to reinvent democracy for its time. It was birthed for freedom, fought a Civil War to extend freedom, waged two world wars to guarantee freedom, and endured a Cold War to protect freedom. Now at its moment of global dominion, while America will certainly apply its military and commercial power for imperial reasons, its *sacred* task, born of its origins in the light, is the extension of freedom to the entire world: freedom of markets, freedom of the individual, freedom of association. If it does not carry out this task of light, like Atlantis, it will surely fall.

At the heart of global issue networks is the conviction that people want to be heard and to participate in developing the rules that govern them. At the global level, this means more than sending national representatives to intergovernmental meetings to deliberate. It means bringing communities of interest together to engage in what political scientist Joshua Cohen calls *deliberative democracy*. Since we are now in an integrating world, democracy must be increasingly inclusive, and it must intentionally bring people together to deliberate upon those rules by which they are called to abide.

This is why network governance is such a compelling vision for the next historical moment. It reinvents democracy at a global level by extending to global concerns the notion of town hall meetings, which lies at the heart of American democracy. It circumvents the need for greater government, especially world government, by channeling the democratic process into voluntary networks of free citizens. This process produces what another political scientist, Jack Critendon, calls the *generative common good,* the notion that when people are included in making the laws, all representing their self-interests, what is generated is the common good. This has been the essence of democracy since its light first burned at the Acropolis twenty-five hundred years ago.

Experiments in network governance have already been made. The International Labor Organization by charter comprises national governments, corporations, and trade unions. For nearly a century, this structure has allowed it to deal with labor issues in a consensual way with the various sectors directly and as peers.

Ruud Lubbers, currently the U.N. High Commissioner for Refugees, actually pioneered issue networks with significant success at a national level in the 1980s when he was prime minister of The Netherlands. In dealing with environmental issues, he developed an approach that brought the environmental and business sectors together to examine and make recommendations to the government. Under his leadership, what were normally competitive and antagonistic sectors of society were brought into a deliberative process that mandated that they come to agreement. Then their consensus recommendations were considered by the Dutch legislature and adopted with modifications. This led to a new form of democracy, wherein the environmental community and the business sector worked together to reach consensus, and on the basis of their recommendations, the government took action. The result was closer collaboration on the part of communities used to being in conflict, and most importantly, legislation that actually solved problems.

Learning from these examples, the United States could take the initiative, for example, in establishing the International Reconstruction Fund that was suggested earlier. It could convene an international gathering of governments, corporations, and civil society actors particularly concerned with the issue of nation building. This group would be empowered to begin the process suggested by Rischard: selecting the best representatives from each sector to come together to gather information, produce specific recommendations, and begin the process of implementation.

The responsibility to protect, the concept suggested by the Commission on Intervention and State Sovereignty, is another area in which the United States, possibly in partnership with the

Canadians and the International Crisis Group, headed by former Australian Foreign Minister Garth Evans, could take leadership by gathering a cross-sectoral group of interested actors to delve more deeply into the issue, refine the findings of the commission, and recommend changes in international law accordingly.

Global issue networks are not rocket science. They are a method for solving global problems by bringing governments, civil society, and the corporate community together in ways appropriate to the kind of solutions our global problems demand. If this were done, what would begin to emerge over time is what Georges Berthoin, first *chef du cabinet* to Jean Monnet and former European chairman of the Trilateral Commission, calls a postinternational or *extranational* system to replace the current nation-state system.

This is a crucial exercise in an integrating world where the central challenge is to develop processes for transboundary communication and collaboration. The essence of an extranational system is the creation of integrating governance mechanisms that bring nations and social sectors together at a higher level of synthesis and interdependence in areas in which they have common concern but in which none of them, acting alone, can solve. Yet by acting together, they all attain their self-interest. Such a shift would be as fundamental as that accomplished eighty years ago by Wilson and sixty years ago by Roosevelt and Truman. Like then, nothing less than the re-envisioning of the entire global system is sufficient to deal with the problems at hand.

Imagine the transposition of values and international respect the United States would experience if instead of fighting the world on global warming, it would ratify the Kyoto protocols, create a global issue network of interested governments, NGOs, and corporations on how most effectively to reduce greenhouse emissions, and then lead the campaign to legitimate this cross-sectoral process.

Imagine if instead of mocking the attempts of international institutions to fight poverty, the U.S. would actually lead an international effort of the wealthiest governments, multilateral institutions, corporations, foundations, and NGOs to guarantee the $50 billion a year during the next twenty years that the World Bank and IMF consider necessary to virtually eliminate poverty and provide clean water, health care, and decent jobs for people in the developing world. Another coalition could be put in place to design the ways that could really deal with alleviating persistent poverty.

Imagine if instead of denigrating and withdrawing from the treaties and protocols seeking to reduce the threat of nuclear, chemical, and biological weapons, small arms and landmines, the United States would lead the international community in reducing stockpiles and stemming proliferation, starting with its own, and initiate a global issue network on innovative ways to ensure global security. The Middle Powers Initiative, a coalition of midsize powers working for nuclear disarmament, could be the seed kernel of such an effort.

At first glance, these propositions might seem preposterous, indeed impossible. Why would the most powerful nation in the world want to get involved in network governance? But sixty years ago, the prospect of forming the United Nations, the Bretton Woods institutions, and the Marshall Plan seemed equally preposterous and daunting. Why would the most powerful nation in the world want to establish the United Nations, or the World Bank, or the IMF? These institutions would never have been created if the United States had stayed within the prewar colonial context. But by re-envisioning the future, by replacing the colonial system with the postimperial system, these institutions that were impossible before the war became the pillars of the new international order after the war.

Establishing Effective Global Governance Before the Deluge

Today, again, what seems impossible is in fact imperative. The current crises are overwhelming, but they must be solved. The system of sovereign nation-states seems eternal but must be transformed. The world is crippled by ineffective government, but it can be delivered by network governance. The world community is critical of the United States, but it requires American leadership.

If the United States would affirm rather than oppose these kinds of measures, it would find the better part of the world ready to begin collaborating, just as both Wilson and Roosevelt did. The world is weary of conflict. It is ready for inspirational leadership and audacious action. The international community is ready to eliminate HIV AIDS, it is ready to take action on global warming, it is ready to eliminate poverty. People are yearning for somebody from somewhere to bring about a more equitable and effective management of the global system.

For America to simply chase the shadows of terrorists and consolidate military hegemony in the face of the totality of our global challenges is to completely miss the point of world affairs in this first decade of the new millennium. If America would protect the world militarily while building cooperative structures, champion the free market while emphasizing the common good, and use its national sovereignty to pioneer network democracy at a global level, it could be not only the greatest empire the world has ever known but also the final empire. The world could be integrated by these actions to such an extent that it could evolve into a mosaic of interconnections and interdependencies in which empire would no longer be needed.

This is not to say that American power would be weakened. As Wilson, Roosevelt, and Truman demonstrated, working to enhance the community of nations only enhances American prestige, influence, and respect. This is the point and paradox of stewardship.

In short, the opportunity before America and the world is this: the League of Nations was established in the ashes of the First World War, the United Nations in the ashes of the Second World War. The challenge now is for the United States to build on these achievements and lead in the building of the next iteration of global governance.

But the United States and the world community must ensure that this time the next global governance regime is implemented proactively, before the catastrophe that will inevitably ensue if our global challenges are not solved.

Can the United States be so inspirational in its leadership of the world that it prevents the kind of catastrophe that produced the other two advances in global governance? Can it prevent the repetition of the most ancient pattern in human history, that real change never actually comes until *after* a crisis? Can the human community break out of this chain of cause and effect?

The next catastrophe, whenever and wherever it arises, will, again, be global. We can be sure of that. It will affect, if not consume, us all. World War I and World War II were both global conflagrations. They affected the whole world. This could happen again, only the next time with more virulence and destructive effect.

Atlantis of old was overwhelmed by an act of the earth, a huge flood that swept Atlantis away. Most of our deepest global problems today are problems of the earth. Perhaps it is from the earth, more than from world war, that America and the world could be victimized, and far more destructively. This is a challenge to which all of us must rise.

It is up to the people of the earth to think consciously for the first time in our history, to engage collectively in the pursuit of light Bacon hoped for, and to become what more recently the theologian Pierre Teilhard de Chardin and the physicist Niels Bohr called "homo noeticus": a new species of humanity that can use its intuition to lead its intelligence, with a heart filled with commitment to light. This notion is in its essence the possibility that, for the first time in history, human beings can break the bonds of history through the power of conscious choice. It is conscious choice, illuminated by light, that breaks the ancient patterns of psyche and soul.

American leadership at this time in history is crucial, provided that America combines its light with its power in such a way that the integrating institutions and mechanisms needed for the effective management of the global system are infused with the same kind of radical democracy with which America itself was founded. A global system of governance, based on inclusive democratic principles, would make impossible the emergence of any other nation-state with imperial ambitions, for the planet will have united as a single matrix of collaborative, self-regulating connections. America's great contribution to history, as the first global democratic empire, could be to make obsolete the necessity for empire.

The challenge to America is whether it can rise to the occasion and provide the kind of global leadership that will seize the opportunities buried in our crises. Midwifing a democratic global system, before going through a global cataclysm, will not be an easy task. If it succeeds, America will gain the accolade of greatness. If it fails, America will be consigned the opprobrium of tragedy.

How America exercises its strength on the global stage during the next several decades will shape the drama of the twenty-first century and the legacy that the United States will leave in the annals of history. America may be the first empire graced with the consciousness to choose its imperial pathway. Given what is at stake for its own people and for the whole world, may it make its choices guided by the wisdom of its past and with the intention of exercising its power in service of the light by which it was founded. What is at stake is nothing less than the foundations of the first planetary civilization.

NOTES

1 AMERICA AND THE WORLD

1 Alexander Motyl, *Imperial Ends: The Decay, Collapse, and Revival of Empires* (New York: Columbia University Press, 2001), p. 4.

2 Michael Doyle, *Empires* (Ithaca, N.Y.: Cornell University Press, 1986), p. 30.

3 Michael Ignatieff, "American Empire," *New York Times Sunday Magazine*, May 1, 2003, p. 22.

4 Thomas Friedman, *The New York Times*, June 4, 2003, op-ed page.

2 A MIGHTY FORTRESS ON SHIFTING SANDS

1 Paul Kennedy, *Financial Times*, Feb. 2, 2002, op-ed page.

2 Josef Joffe, "Who's Afraid of Mr. Big?" *The National Interest*, Summer 2001, p. 49.

3 Stephen Brooks and William Wohlforth, "American Primacy in Perspective," *Foreign Affairs*, July-Aug. 2002, p. 31.

4 Henry Kissinger, *Does America Need a Foreign Policy?* (New York: Simon & Schuster, 2001), p. 17.

5 Kissinger, *Foreign Policy*, p. 18.

6 Kissinger, *Foreign Policy*, p. 19.

7 Kissinger, *Foreign Policy*, p. 19.

8 Kissinger, *Foreign Policy*, p. 19.

9 Kissinger, *Foreign Policy*, p. 20.

10 Kissinger, *Foreign Policy*, p. 21.

11 Jean-François Rischard, *High Noon: Twenty Global Problems, Twenty Years to Solve Them* (New York: Basic Books, 2002), p. 157.

12 George Soros, *On Globalization* (New York: Public Affairs, 2002), pg. 6.

3   AMERICA'S JOURNEY TO EMPIRE

1 General Henry M. Shelton, *Joint Vision 2020* (Washington, D.C.: U.S. Department of Defense, 1996), p. 4.

2 "The National Security Strategy of the United States," White House press release, Sept. 20, 2002, p. 1.

3 "National Security Strategy of the United States," p. 1.

4 "National Security Strategy of the United States," p. 2.

5 "National Security Strategy of the United States," p. 10.

6 "National Security Strategy of the United States," p. 10.

7 "National Security Strategy of the United States," p. 21.

8 "Defense Planning Guidance" (Washington, D.C.: U.S. Department of Defense, 1992).

9 Zalmay Khalizad, *From Containment to Global Leadership?: America & the World After the Cold War* (Washington, D.C.: Rand/United States Air Force, 1995), p. 13.

10 Khalizad, *From Containment to Global Leadership?*, p. 41.

11 Hugh Dick (ed.), *Francis Bacon: Selected Writings* (New York: Random House, 1958).

12 Dick, *Francis Bacon*, p. 564.

13 Dick, *Francis Bacon*, p. 570.

14 Julian P. Boyd (ed.), *The Papers of Thomas Jefferson*, Vol. 12 (Princeton, N.J.: Princeton University Press, 1955), p. 28.

15 Mead, *Special Providence*, p. 8.

4   THE ROOTS OF AMERICAN PREEMINENCE

1 Walter Russell Mead, *Special Providence*, (New York: Knopf, 2001) p. 129.

2 Mead, *Special Providence*, p. 125.

3 Martin Walker, "What Kind of Empire?" *Wilson Quarterly*, Summer 2002, p. 44.

4 Walker, "What Kind of Empire?" p. 47.

5 Walker, "What Kind of Empire?" p. 47.

6 Percy Bysshe Shelley, "On the Manners of the Ancients," in William Durant, *The Story of Civilization, Vol. II: The Life of Greece* (New York: Simon & Schuster, 1966), p. 245.

7 Edith Hamilton, *The Greek Way* (New York: Time Books, 1963), p. x.

8 Durant, *Story of Civilization, Vol. II*, p. 254.

9 Alexander Hamilton, John Jay, James Madison, *The Federalist Papers* (New York: Random House/Modern Library, 1937), no. 10.

10 Hamilton, Jay, Madison, *The Federalist Papers*, no. 51.

11 Hamilton, Jay, Madison, *The Federalist Papers*, no. 51.

12 Andrew Bacevich, "New Rome, New Jerusalem," *Wilson Quarterly*, Summer 2002, p. 52.

13 Bacevich, "New Rome, New Jerusalem," p. 52.

14 Paul M. Kennedy, *New York Times*, Mar. 31, 2002, op-ed page.

5   EMPIRE AND ITS DISCONTENTS

1 Ignatieff, "American Empire," p. 27.

2 Ignatieff, "American Empire," p. 50.

3 Robert Kagan, *Of Paradise and Power* (New York: Knopf, 2003), p. 3.

4 Kagan, *Of Paradise and Power*, p. 58.

5 Kagan, *Of Paradise and Power*, p. 76.

6   THE RISE AND FALL OF EMPIRES

1 Durant, *Story of Civilization, Vol. II*, p. 121.

2 Durant, *Story of Civilization, Vol. II*, p. 219.

3 Irwin St. John Tucker, *A History of Imperialism* (New York: Rand School of Science, 1920), p. 5.

4 Durant, *Story of Civilization, Vol. II*, p. 218.

5 Walker, "What Kind of Empire?", p. 42.

6 Durant, *Story of Civilization, Vol. I, Our Oriental Heritage*, p. 222.

7 Thucydides, *The Peloponnesian War, Vol. II* [Rex Warner, trans.] (New York: Penguin Books, 1954), p. 65.

8 Edward Gibbon, *The History of the Decline and Fall of the Roman Empire* [abridged] (New York: Penguin, 2000), p. 10.

9 Gibbon, *Decline and Fall of the Roman Empire*, p. 435.

7   THE ROMAN ACHIEVEMENT

1 Gibbon, *Decline and Fall of the Roman Empire*, p. 83.

2 Durant, *Story of Civilization, Vol. III, Caesar and Christ*, p. 408.

3 Durant, *Story of Civilization, Vol. III*, p. 409.

4 Durant, *Story of Civilization, Vol. III*, p. 409.

5 Durant, *Story of Civilization, Vol. III*, p. 413.

6 Durant, *Story of Civilization, Vol. III*, p. 416.

7 Durant, *Story of Civilization, Vol. III*, p. 416.

8 Durant, *Story of Civilization, Vol. III*, p. 420.

9 Durant, *Story of Civilization, Vol. III*, p. 422.

10 Durant, *Story of Civilization, Vol. III*, p. 424.

11 Durant, *Story of Civilization, Vol. III*, p. 422.

12 Durant, *Story of Civilization, Vol. III*, p. 426.

13 Durant, *Story of Civilization, Vol. III*, p. 426.

14 Durant, *Story of Civilization, Vol. III*, p. 427.

15 Durant, *Story of Civilization, Vol. III*, p. 432.

16 Durant, *Story of Civilization, Vol. III*, p. 448.

17 Durant, *Story of Civilization, Vol. III*, p. 670.

18 Durant, *Story of Civilization, Vol. III*, p. 670.

19 Durant, *Story of Civilization, Vol. III*, p. 670.

8 AMERICA AT THE CHOICE POINT

1 Michael Glennon, "What's Law Got to Do with It?" *Wilson Quarterly*, Summer 2002, p. 72.

2 Walker, "What Kind of Empire?" p. 42.

3 Elias Canetti, *Crowds and Power* [Carol Stewart, trans.] (London: Penguin Books, 1973), p. 166.

4 Zbigniew Brzezinski, *New York Times*, Sept. 1, 2002, op-ed page.

5 Brzezinski, *New York Times*, op-ed page.

9 THE FINAL EMPIRE

1 Michael Lind, "Toward a Global Society of States," *Wilson Quarterly*, Summer 2002, p. 61.

2 Lind, "Global Society," p. 66.

3 Sebastian Mallaby, "The Reluctant Imperialist," *Foreign Affairs*, Mar.-Apr. 2002, p. 7.

4 Mallaby, "Reluctant Imperialist," p. 7.

5 Anne-Marie Slaughter, *Washington Post*, Apr. 20, 2003, op-ed page.

6 Gareth Evans and Mohamed Sahnoun, "The Responsibility to Protect," *Foreign Affairs*, Nov.-Dec. 2002, p. 101. Evans and Sahnoun were the co-chairs of the International Commission on Intervention and State Sovereignty.

7 Soros, *On Globalization*, p. 165.

8 Soros, *On Globalization*, p. 178.

9 Soros, *On Globalization*, p. 165.

INDEX

JIM GARRISON was born in Szechuan Province, China, in 1951 to Baptist missionaries. He lived with his family in Taiwan from 1953 to 1965, after which they settled permanently in San Jose, California. While attending Abraham Lincoln High School there, he was twice elected student body president.

Garrison began college at Pepperdine University (1969–70), attended the University of Tel Aviv as an exchange student in 1972, and received a B.A. magna cum laude in World History from Santa Clara University in 1973. He then went on to obtain a double M.T.S. in Christology and History of Religion from Harvard Divinity School (1975) and a Ph.D. in Philosophical Theology from Cambridge University (1982).

As a student, Garrison actively opposed the Vietnam war and became engaged in the antinuclear movement and in the citizen diplomacy movement to reduce tensions between the United States and the Soviet Union. He founded two organizations dealing with these issues: The Radiation and Health Information Service and East West Reach. In 1980, he published his first book, *The Plutonium Culture* (SCM). This was followed by *The Darkness of God: Theology After Hiroshima* (SCM, 1982); *The Russian Threat: Myths and Realities* (Gateway Books, 1983); *The New*

Diplomats (Resurgence Press, 1984); and *Civilization and the Transformation of Power* (Paraview Press, 2000).

From 1986 to 1990, Garrison served as executive director of the Esalen Institute Soviet American Exchange Program, which engaged in private sector diplomacy with Soviet counterparts in a variety of sectors. In 1991, he founded the International Foreign Policy Association in collaboration with Georgian President Edward Shevardnadze and former Secretary of State George Schultz, focusing on providing humanitarian relief for the former Soviet republics. In 1992, at the behest of Mikhail Gorbachev, Garrison founded and became the president of the Gorbachev Foundation/USA.

These two organizations set the stage for the establishment in 1995 of the State of the World Forum, a San Francisco-based non-profit institution created to establish a global network of leaders dedicated to those principles, values, and actions necessary to guide humanity toward a more sustainable global civilization. With President Gorbachev as its convening chairman and Garrison as its president, the Forum has brought leaders from around the world and a spectrum of disciplines to its annual and regional forums to deliberate upon and take action concerning issues of global concern.

Additionally, the Forum has launched and directed a number of action-oriented strategic initiatives across a range of areas, many of which have become their own organizations. These include the Global Security Institute, the Coexistence Network, Global Equal Access, the Whole Child Initiative, and the Ethical Globalization Initiative. The State of the World Forum also convened the Commission on Globalization in 2000.

Garrison is active in Democratic Party politics and ran for Congress in Silicon Valley in 1988. He is also active in Mosaic Networks, a global business development company, of which he is a partner. He currently lives in Mill Valley, California, with his wife Claire and their two sons, Luke and Zachary.

ABOUT STATE OF THE WORLD FORUM

TRANSFORMING CONVERSATIONS THAT MATTER INTO
    ACTIONS THAT MAKE A DIFFERENCE   State of the World
    Forum (the Forum) was established by Jim Garrison in 1995 to
    develop a global leadership network across a multiplicity of disci-
    plines and from around the world dedicated to working toward a
    sustainable global civilization. The Forum was an offshoot of the
    Gorbachev Foundation/USA, which Garrison founded in 1992, in
    partnership with Mikhail Gorbachev, Senator Alan Cranston, who
    served as chairman of the board of trustees, and George Shultz,
    secretary of state under President Ronald Reagan, who served as
    chairman of the board of advisors.

    Mr. Gorbachev serves as the convening chairman of State of
    the World Forum. An international group of leaders serve with
    him as co-chairs, including Askar Akaev, Oscar Arias, Jean-
    Bertrand Aristide, James Baker, Tansu Çiller, Sonia Gandhi, Jane
    Goodall, Ruud Lubbers, Federico Mayor, Thabo Mbeki, Gertrude
    Mongella, Yasuhiro Nakasone, Wally N'Dow, Her Majesty Queen
    Noor of Jordan, José Ramos-Horta, Jehan Sadat, George Shultz
    (retired as co-chair in 1998), Maurice Strong (retired in 1996), Ted
    Turner, Desmond Tutu, Elie Wiesel, Marian Wright Edelman,
    and Muhammad Yunus.

Under the auspices of this esteemed group, the Forum has convened a series of international conferences that have served to connect leaders and thinkers who may not traditionally interact. What has emerged from these gatherings is a community of influence leaders representing a wide spectrum of disciplines, regions, and cultures who come together united by a shared sense of responsibility for the human future. The first State of the World Forum was convened in San Francisco in 1995 and featured a debate that was carried live worldwide on CNN between Mr. Gorbachev, Margaret Thatcher, and George Bush, Sr., on the future of the United Nations.

Since then, a series of international gatherings has been organized with selected international partners. In 1996, a partnership was established with then-Governor Vicente Fox in Guanajuato, Mexico, to examine the fundamental trends shaping the future of Latin America. This event resulted in the establishment in Guanajuato of a Grameen-type bank and the Human Development Center.

In 1997, another partnership was established with the Human Development Center to convene an event in Bhurbon, Pakistan, to examine human development in the twenty-first century, producing the Bhurbon Declaration. Also in 1997, an event was organized in the European Parliament in Brussels on the issue of endocrine-disrupting chemicals and their impact on human health. The conference led to a Draft Parliamentary Recommendation on Endocrine-Disrupting Chemicals, adopted in 1998 by the European Commission, to focus increased European governmental, scientific, and industry attention on this serious issue.

In 1999, an international gathering in Belfast and Dublin was convened to discuss the challenges of coexistence and community building in a global age. During the conference, Oracle Corporation donated one hundred Internet-ready computers to four Catholic, Protestant, and integrated schools in Belfast to facilitate what it called "coexistence through computing." Also in 1999, the Forum hosted in Monterrey, Mexico, the first State of the World Forum for Emerging Leaders entirely organized and led by youth.

During the event, the youth launched the Emerging Leaders Program, an organization led, staffed, and funded entirely by youth.

In 2000, the Forum convened a major gathering in New York under the theme "Globalization: Convening the Community of Stakeholders," timed to coincide with the United Nations Millennium Summit of Heads of State. A dozen heads of state and over two thousand leaders representing governments, nongovernmental organizations, organized protest groups, corporations, trade unions, international financial institutions, multilateral agencies, the science and technology sector, religious communities, academia, and the media came together to discuss the major issues related to globalization and global governance. BBC World Television broadcast two debates live from the conference to worldwide audiences. This conference established the Commission on Globalization, the mission of which is to convene a leadership network to recommend policy alternatives and work together to implement constructive changes in the global system. Over 250 world leaders from government, civil society, and business participate in the Commission, convening conferences on different issues of concern and developing collaborative actions on specific issues of policy reform.

In 2003, the Commission on Globalization organized a conference in Brussels on the theme "National Sovereignty and Universal Challenges: Choices for the World After Iraq," with particular focus on the phenomenon of U.S. power, the deepening fissures in the transatlantic alliance, and the lessons that can be learned from the development of the European Union. As a result of this gathering, the Forum partnered with American Express, Booz Allen Hamilton, and the International Chamber of Commerce, among others, to launch the Integral Governance Initiative to examine the complexities of the new operating reality and to develop cross-sectoral approaches to global governance.

Since 1995, the Forum has catalyzed and incubated a number of strategic initiatives and partnerships that have matured into their own independent organizations, including the following:

COEXISTENCE NETWORK. Established as *The Coexistence and Community Building Initiative* by the Abraham Fund and State of the State of the World Forum in 1996 to convene high-level groups of policy analysts, practitioners, educators, and theorists to deliberate on how to enhance international interest in coexistence and community building and to make specific recommendations to governments and educational institutions. During the Belfast Conference organized by the Forum in May 1999, the initiative launched *A Plan of Action for the 21st Century,* a platform providing the basis for an international coexistence movement. The Coexistence Initiative spun off and became an independent nonprofit organization, the Coexistence Network, in 1999.

ETHICAL GLOBALISATION INITIATIVE. Established in 2002 by Mary Robinson, former U.N. High Commissioner for Human Rights, in partnership with the Aspen Institute, the International Council on Human Rights Policy, and State of the World Forum. This initiative focuses on policy development and practical applications aimed at more effectively integrating human rights norms and standards into governmental and corporate practices, with a particular emphasis on Africa. It established a major partnership with Columbia University in fall 2003 with a commitment to connect human rights, human development, and human security.

GLOBAL EQUAL ACCESS. Established by Solaria Corporation, State of the World Forum, and WorldSpace Corporation in 1999 to bring information affluence to the world's dispossessed by delivering critically needed information to underserved regions of the world through digital satellite audio/multimedia broadcasting, solar energy, and other appropriate technologies. This strategic initiative became a nonprofit organization in 2001 and is now working with UNDP and the U.N. Foundation to create a region-wide Digital Broadcast Initiative designed to reach one thousand community-based village sites in South Asia and Southeast Asia.

GLOBAL SECURITY INSTITUTE. Established by Senator Alan Cranston and Mikhail Gorbachev in 1995 as the Nuclear Weapons Elimination Initiative to contribute to the creation of a national and global debate on nuclear weapons and the need for their worldwide abolition. A number of declarations and a series of public statements by civilian and military leaders were produced calling for reductions in nuclear armaments. In 1999, the Nuclear Weapons Elimination Initiative became the Global Security Institute, which operates as an independent nonprofit organization.

WHOLE CHILD INITIATIVE. Established by Dr. Jane Goodall with Marian Wright Edelman in 1996 to convene experts in the fields of child development, psychology, and education with program leaders working at the grassroots level globally with children. It has as its mission to identify, support, and promote effective community-based programs worldwide that improve the well-being of children. To date, funding and support have been given to some fifty grassroots projects in Africa, Latin America, and Asia. Lessons learned through partnering with programs that are holistic in their approach, integrating local knowledge and culture, and enriched by intergenerational wisdom, will be used to empower and connect existing programs and to strengthen the knowledge base of the next generation of programs for children. In 2003, the Whole Child Initiative became its own independent nonprofit organization.

As globalization takes root, power is being democratized even as, in many quarters, democracy is being imperiled. New actors are emerging and must be taken into account and respected. All are demanding seats at the table of governance. Gorbachev Foundation/USA and State of the World Forum address these challenges by bringing diverse actors together for sustained dialogue, deliberation, and collaborative action. This is the basis on which these organizations were established and it is the mission to which they are dedicated.

Gangs of America
The Rise of Corporate Power & the Disabling of Democracy

Ted Nace

Through a series of fascinating stories populated by colorful personalities, *Gangs of America* details the rise of corporate power in America. Driven to answer the central question of how corporations got more rights than people, Ted Nace delves deep into the origins of this institution that has become a hallmark of the modern age. He synthesizes the latest research with a compelling historical narrative to tell the rich tale of the rise of corporate power in America.

Hardcover, 280 pages • ISBN 1-57675-260-7 • Item #52607 $24.95

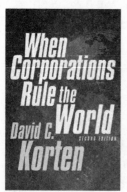

When Corporations Rule the World
Second Edition

David C. Korten

David Korten offers an alarming exposé of the devastating consequences of economic globalization and a passionate message of hope in this well-reasoned, extensively researched analysis. He documents the human and environmental consequences of economic globalization and explains why human survival depends on a community-based, people-centered alternative.

Paperback, 400 pages • ISBN 1-887208-04-6
Item #08046 $15.95

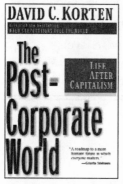

The Post-Corporate World
Life After Capitalism

David C. Korten

The Post-Corporate World presents readers with both a profound challenge and an empowering sense of hope. It is an extensively researched, powerfully argued, eye-opening critique of how today's corporate capitalism is destroying the things of real value in the world—like cancer destroys life—including practical alternatives that will help restore health to markets, democracy, and every day life.

Paperback, 300 pages • ISBN 1-887208-03-8 • Item #08038 $19.95

Berrett-Koehler Publishers
PO Box 565, Williston, VT 05495-9900
Call toll-free! **800-929-2929** 7 am-9 pm Eastern Standard Time
Or fax your order to 802-864-7627
For fastest service order online: **www.bkconnection.com**

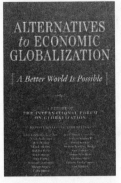

Alternatives to Economic Globalization
A Better World Is Possible

The International Forum on Globalization

Alternatives to Economic Globalization is the culmination of a three-year project to define alternatives to the current corporate model of globalization. Written by 18 leading thinkers from around the world, this official consensus report of the International Forum on Globalization, lays out alternatives to the corporate globalization more fully, specifically, and thoughtfully than has ever been done before.

Paperback, 350 pages • ISBN 1-57675-204-6 • Item #52046 $15.95

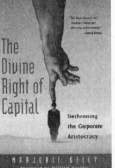

The Divine Right of Capital
Dethroning the Corporate Aristocracy

Marjorie Kelly

In *The Divine Right of Capital,* Marjorie Kelly argues that focusing on the interests of stockholders to the exclusion of everyone else's interests is a form of discrimination based on property or wealth. She shows how this bias is held by our institutional structures, much as they once held biases against blacks and women. *The Divine Right of Capital* shows how to design more equitable alternatives—new property rights, new forms of corporate governance, new ways of looking at corporate performance—that build on both free-market and democratic principles.

Paperback, 288 pages • ISBN 1-57675-237-2 • Item #52372 $17.95

Affluenza
The All-Consuming Epidemic

John de Graaf, David Wann, and Thomas H. Naylor

Based on two highly acclaimed PBS documentaries, *Affluenza* uses the metaphor of a disease to tackle a very serious subject: the damage done—to our health, our families, our communities, and our environment—by the obsessive quest for material gain that has been the core principle of the American Dream. The authors explore the origins of affluenza, detail the symptoms of the disease, and describe number of treatments options that offer hope for recovery.

Paperback, 288 pages • ISBN 1-57675-199-6 • Item #51996 $16.95

Berrett-Koehler Publishers
PO Box 565, Williston, VT 05495-9900
Call toll-free! **800-929-2929** 7 am-9 pm Eastern Standard Time

Or fax your order to 802-864-7627
For fastest service order online: **www.bkconnection.com**